Disciples of Christ
in the 21st Century

Disciples of Christ in the 21st Century

edited by Michael Kinnamon

CBP Press

St. Louis, Missouri

Unless otherwise indicated, all scripture quotations are from the Revised Standard Version of the Bible, copyrighted 1946, 1952, © 1971, 1973, by the Division of Christian Education of the National Council of Churches of Christ in the United States of America.

Library of Congress Cataloging-in-Publication Data

Disciples of Christ in the 21st century / edited by Michael Kinnamon p. cm.
    Proceedings of a conference held at Christian Theological Seminary, March 29—April 1, 1987.
    ISBN 0-8272-0616-X : $6.95
    1. Christian Church (Disciples of Christ)—Congresses.
I. Kinnamon, Michael.
BX7321.2.D57 1988   87-25634
286.6'3—dc19   CIP

Contents

Preface

Has the Christian Church (Disciples of Christ) in recent years lost some of its vitality, direction, and sense of distinctive "identity" —along with a good number of its members? Many Disciples think so and feel that the question must now be addressed with clarity and urgency.

Such was also the conviction behind a most unusual conference sponsored by the students and faculty of Christian Theological Seminary (Indianapolis) in the spring of 1987. Our hope for the conference was revealed in its title: "Christians Only But Not the Only Christians; Reappraising the Disciples Tradition for the 21st Century."

Part of the church in contemporary America has seemed content to let Christian faith be but one priority among many in the lives of its members; another part has regarded its hold on truth as absolute, denying alternative ways to faithfulness. Can we be "Christians only," pointing to the gospel of Jesus Christ as the center from which our lives receive their meaning, while still acknowledging that we are "not the only Christians," that we have no monopoly on understanding God's will?

If Disciples were able to hold these together, to be both "evangelical" and "ecumenical," would we recover a part of our distinctive witness? Can we learn to look afresh at the Disciples tradition for guidance without becoming enslaved to dated conceptions of the church and its mission? Can we adequately anticipate challenges awaiting us in the 21st Century and begin to address them out of our heritage? Obviously a single conference could not answer all of these questions! But we hoped that by focusing on them, by providing a much needed opportunity for theological dialogue, the conference might serve as a stimulus for renewal among Disciples.

The planning committee sent special letters of invitation to various leaders, lay and ordained, in the denomination, but the event was also publicized in *The Disciple* and was intended to be open. We had anticipated between 150 and 200 participants for what was, after all, an "unofficial" conference. But registration eventually exceeded 550, with participants coming from all parts of the nation. A high percentage was ordained, including a great many local pastors. Approximately 30 percent were women. Special effort was made to encourage representation from diverse theological perspectives (especially conservative evangelical), and this effort was quite successful. Far less successful were attempts to encourage the participation of black and Hispanic church leaders. "For precisely this reason," said the conference final report, "we are aware that our conference has been far from ideal. . . . The wisdom of the wider church body must be added to our beginnings."

Publicity for the conference emphasized that this was not to be a "continuing education event" but a "working conference." Registrants were asked to specify a working group (ministry, worship, authority, evangelism, congregational life and discipline, structure, global mission, or the church and social transformation) and to remain in it throughout the conference. This meant more than ten hours of open conversation and drafting. In order to focus these working group discussions, three background papers were prepared for each group and distributed in advance—one dealing with what we can learn from the Disciples heritage on that particular issue, one with present strengths and weaknesses, and one with possible directions for future growth. These papers have already been published in the July 1987 issue of *Midstream* and are available from the Disciples Council on Christian Unity.

Our committee had hoped that each working group would produce a brief statement or report that might be shared with the wider church. But, after the first day of the three-day event, many participants obviously doubted that it could be done. "There isn't enough time." "We come from such different starting points." "We're not experienced in this kind of dialogue." Most stayed with it, however, and by the end of the second day, drafting groups were spread throughout the seminary. By the third day, when the reports were read and commented on in plenary, the frustration had generally disappeared. In the preface to the group

8

reports, the participants affirmed that "in worship and intensive discussion, we have experienced the energy which comes through commitment to dialogue and renewal. We have attempted to speak truthfully in love to and with each other about issues central to our common life—and it has been exciting!"

The reports of the eight working groups, along with the preface approved by the whole conference, are printed in this volume. They are not polished examples of academic research; they follow no standardized format. But they do show what problems serious, informed Disciples identify when they come together to think about the church; and, in some cases, they offer suggestions for dealing with them. Congregations and regional gatherings may find that these reports provide a useful starting point for their own discussions.

Participants did not spend all of their time, however, in working groups. Three plenary sessions helped to hold the conference together by providing input on themes of general concern. James Duke and Julia Marie Brown addressed the topic "Issues Confronting the Church in the 21st Century: What Can Disciples Contribute?" Three speakers—William Paulsell, William Nottingham, and Clark Williamson—approached from refreshingly different perspectives the question, "Where Should Disciples Look for Renewal?" And Nadia Lahutsky and T. Garrott Benjamin dealt with the thorny problem, "Can an Ecumenical Church Be Evangelistic? Can an Evangelistic Church Be Ecumenical?" In addition, the conference opened and closed with sermons by Joe Jones and Joan Campbell. (The various speakers are identified at the beginnings of their addresses and sermons printed in this volume.)

These addresses and sermons are, in my estimation, uniformly excellent. They represent a wide range of Disciples life—local pastors, educators, national executives, ecumenical workers—and provide evidence of genuine intellectual vitality in our denomination. All nine sermons and addresses are printed in this volume.

I will not attempt to summarize the material that follows, but I do want to mention one theme or concern that surfaced repeatedly in the reports, addresses, background papers, and conversations. Disciples, we said to one another, must learn to affirm diversity (theological as well as racial and cultural diversity) while still insisting that freedom in Christ does not mean "we can believe and do whatever we please." Our proper refusal to demand that others conform to us does not release us from the obligation that we be conformed to Christ in our life and mission. Ways must be found, said different groups, to recover a sense of "discipline" (defined, at one point, as nurture and ordering rather than correction or punishment) in our congregational life and the possibility of "teaching authority" in the church as a whole; but we must do so in ways consistent with our traditional emphasis on dispersed "covenantal" authority. And all of this, in turn, will demand greater biblical literacy, more careful attention to spirituality and worship, increased global and historical awareness, and (perhaps foundational to the rest) a greater willingness to talk seriously to each other about basic issues of the faith. Clark Williamson put it forcefully in his plenary address:

> When the church quits thinking theologically, when it ceases to discipline its life by critical self-reflection, it tends to lose its ecclesial existence and to proceed aimlessly toward becoming a ritualistic, alienated association of people providing such services as the relief of psychic distress and institutional maintenance. One source of our renewal lies in recapturing the ability to think theologically about our common life. If this conference helps such thinking among Disciples, it will have been a success.

Michael Kinnamon

Christians Only But Not the Only Christians

Reappraising the Disciples Tradition for the 21st Century

Christian Theological Seminary
March 29—April 1, 1987

From March 29 to April 1, 1987, more than five hundred Christians, most of us members of the Christian Church (Disciples of Christ), gathered at Christian Theological Seminary to reappraise the Disciples tradition for the 21st Century. We have been brought together by our love for this church with its rich heritage of witness and service and by our concern that the church we love is facing difficult questions regarding its distinctive identity and mission. This may well be a crucial moment for Disciples.

Throughout this conference we joyfully affirmed that we are "Christians Only But Not the Only Christians." In worship and intensive discussion, we experienced the energy that comes through a common commitment to dialogue and renewal. We attempted to speak truthfully in love to and with one another about issues central to our common life—and it was exciting!

The heart of the conference was eight working groups dealing with themes of ministry, worship, authority, evangelism, congregational life and discipline, structure, global mission, and the church and social transformation. In order to stimulate and focus the working group conversations, three background papers were prepared for each group and sent to participants in advance—one dealing with what we can learn from our heritage on this issue, one on present strengths and weaknesses, and one on directions for future growth. Each group produced a statement stemming from its conversations, which may be of use to other parts of the church as they consider these important themes.

11

We were also challenged, through a series of addresses and sermons, to reflect more generally on who we are and where we are headed. Particularly exciting was the way these speakers went beyond simply naming our problems to lift up images and visions of the church we are called to be. Among many other things, we heard the following:

When the church quits thinking theologically, when it ceases to discipline its life by critical self-reflection, it tends to lose its ecclesial existence and to proceed aimlessly toward becoming a ritualistic, alienated association of people providing such services as the relief of psychic distress and institutional maintenance. One source of our renewal assuredly lies in recapturing the ability to think theologically about our common life. (Clark Williamson)

I suggest to you that "the church is that community of persons called into being by the gospel of Jesus Christ to witness in word and deed to the living God for the benefit of the world." . . . The church has been given one comprehensive and essential task: *to witness* in word and deed to the living God for the benefit of the world. However warm may be our fellowship, however comfortable our gatherings, if we are not engaged in witness, then quite simply we are not the church of Jesus Christ. There is no blunter way to put it. The Scriptures tell us that we have this ministry by the mercy of God in order that we might provide an open statement of the truth as ambassadors for Christ. A failure to recover this vital and dynamic sense of witness as the mission of the church will guarantee continued futility, despair, and hand-wringing. (Joe Jones)

There are still Christians who sense that the church is called to a ministry beyond self-defense and self-indulgence. But they suffer a crisis of confidence. Too conservative for some, too radical for others, they find themselves increasingly marginalized, and left to haggle over what it all means. The haggling does nothing to improve their lot. The century ahead looms as their time of trial. Quite naturally many will say that the church needs to recover its confidence. But the confidence it recovers must be of a very special sort. Hence I would prefer to argue that the church is in need of reminders that real confidence comes only from the gospel that casts out fear. (James Duke)

The Christian Church (Disciples of Christ) has a distinctive identity worth preserving. We have been a church characterized by attention to the biblical witness (and not any particular tradition about the Bible), by an orientation to reasonableness (that is, a willingness to use methods of

12

human thought to understand the gospel), and by our commitment to the unity of the church (rooted in our aching sense that we are not the whole). These three aspects of our identity share, it would seem, the common root in our conviction that our ways may not be God's ways and thus they must always be open to critique. The common wisdom today is that a church cannot be ecumenical and evangelistic, that we will sacrifice one or the other. Wrong! Evangelism and ecumenism are related and shared aspects of the one faith and integral to who we are; to give up either of them is to give up our identity. (Nadia Lahutsky)

We must resist the tendency to have Protestantism, let alone Disciples, defined by sectarians. That was the problem in the beginning! There are *ecumenical* conservative evangelicals, and the World Council of Churches is full of them from the Lutheran Church of Norway to the Greek Orthodox, or the Pentecostals of Chile. Our DOM works with Roman Catholics in Brazil and the Christian Apostolic Holiness Church in Zion in Swaziland, not because they are liberal, but because they understand the oneness of the church of Jesus Christ. . . . There will be no renewal of the Disciples by lowering our ecumenical commitments. Intelligence has led us to the commitment to the wholeness of the church, so that we use the expression "not the only Christians," and we must see what a victory this has been. (William Nottingham)

The church of the 21st Century will be confronted with one critical theological issue, which will give birth and substance to a number of related issues. It will not be a new phenomenon, rather a growing one, which is the sin of self-interest or plain selfishness from an individual, as well as a collective perspective. The sin of self-interest, which leads to self-idolatry, breeds issues such as economic oppression, militarism, racism, and sexism. The church of the 21st Century will be concerned with initiating a ministry that will be concerned with evangelism and conversion that is qualitative, effecting deeper and deeper changes in the heart of persons, which will result in changes of sinful structures, economic systems and political patterns in the global community. The Christian Church (Disciples of Christ) may contribute to decreasing the suffering that will exist in the 21st Century by teaching a Christian faith that has the capacity to liberate and transform the hearts of people. (Julia Marie Brown)

I fervently hope that Christ will not say to me, "Sell what you have, give to the poor and come follow me." I find it impossible to live by, "Take no thought for the morrow." I am made very uncomfortable by the admonition, "If anyone would come after me, let that person deny the self and come follow me." But these ideas are part of the gospel. Jesus does not bless the middle-class ideals of American life—upward

13

mobility, prosperity, and needless consumption. We must not measure the church by those standards. We need to take more seriously the radicalism of Jesus and try to understand it. If the church is successful by worldly standards, it may be because we have compromised the gospel and been unfaithful to its demands on us. (William Paulsell)

We need to move from the idea of "melting pot" to the reality of "sanctified salad." A "sanctified salad" represents Christians who bring their individuality and differences together to enhance unity and not to erode it. A salad becomes a salad only when the individual ingredients stand on their own in the same bowl. The modern church seems to want its "onions" and "cucumbers" to be the same. This is self-defeating. Our churches are full of "look-alikes" that worship alike, whine alike, and decline alike. Instead, we need to inspire inclusiveness and delight in diversity, realizing that it contributes to our tradition as a people who sincerely believe and practice "unity without uniformity." The sooner we do this the closer we will be to reflecting the will of God for the church in our time—a "world house" church that demonstrates unconditional love without regard to (but regard for the interpretations and perspectives of) race, color, creed, or national origin; where Jew and Gentile, African and Afrikaaner, master and servant, male and female; white, red, yellow, and brown; have and have not, educated and uneducated, degree and no degree, Ph.D. and "no D," can sit together at the Master's Table. Anything less than this kind of inclusiveness winds up leaving the church parochial, provincial, and powerless. (T. Garrott Benjamin)

Can we, who live where decisions are made daily that deal in the life and death for millions, be passionate about God's future? If we appear to be afraid of passion, there is good reason. A holy passion is a mix of joy with agony, of suffering with security, of love with betrayal. Passion crowds out fear. Faith is required to be passionate, for it makes absolutely no sense in an affluent and increasingly secular society, a society where suffering and sacrifice are to be avoided (and if they cannot be avoided must be hidden). But without sacrifice life loses volume and weight. An unbearable lightness of being is the outcome, and with a featherweight existence *not only sacrifice but joy becomes impossible.* When passion is missing, death, not life, dominates. To be passionate is to risk suffering and to find joy. It may be the only way for the Spirit to enter our complacent souls. *God's love for us is not platonic!* We dare not offer less to those who share this planet with us. Possibly, just possibly, if we become passionate about God's future, it will creep into all our acts of praise; and our work and worship and our prayer life will be renewed and rekindled; and we will be reborn. (Joan Campbell)

14

One strong affirmation coming from this experience is that the church must be an inclusive community, that we need one another—women and men, lay and ordained, of whatever color or language—in order to be more true to the church God wills. For precisely this reason we are aware that our conference was far from ideal. Laypersons were underrepresented, along with blacks, Hispanics, Asians, and other minority groups within the Disciples. The wisdom of the wider church body must be added to our beginnings.

Still, we think that this kind of conference (especially if it were to become more inclusive) could serve as an effective model for promoting theological discussion and renewal throughout the church. We urge regions and congregations to consider fostering theological dialogue around the issues listed above or others that Disciples need to address. The commitment to talk seriously with one another about our faith is a part of who we are.

Throughout this meeting we sensed a genuine vitality, a willingness to think creatively *together* about our mission for the coming century. We confess that it is God who gives this power of new life and who calls us as individuals and community to continual growth. To God be glory for ever and ever!

Working Group Reports

Authority

The issue of authority is an important one for the Christian Church (Disciples of Christ) because of the origin and history of our church and because of our desire to clarify our identity as we turn our attention to the 21st Century. We are a people who possess a deep passion for Christian freedom, moved and motivated by the redeeming and liberating power of the gospel. At the same time, we are a people who desire to bear witness to the gospel in a way that is authentic and authoritative. Therefore, this statement is offered to the church in hopes that as we continue to reflect upon the nature of authority in the community of faith, a better sense of identity might develop in the hearts and lives of our people.

The ultimate authority in the life of the church is the presence of the living God expressed to us in Christ. Scripture, Old and New Testament, has authority in the life of the church as it bears witness to the presence of the living God in Christ. Scripture is interpreted in a dynamic relationship with the traditions of Israel and the church and our own experience of living by faith.

As the church listens to scripture, there will always be a creative tension between the historical-cultural nature of scripture (the Bible is an ancient document) and our need to experience the presence of the living God in Christ (the Bible points to a divine reality beyond itself). The church, therefore, is called to interpret scripture courageously, realizing that any interpretive effort is fallible because we are fallible.

For Disciples, the authority of the church must be understood in terms of covenant. Our understanding of covenant is inherently confessional because it is always God who initiates that covenant. In response to this divine authority, we are called into covenant, which is, by the inner compulsion of God's call, wholly transformative. In Christ's suffering love, we understand ourselves to be more than a human community, having been called into the mystery of God's grace.

Because God relates to us with trust, compassion, and forgiveness, we are compelled to relate to God and to one another with trust, compassion, and forgiveness. In covenant, authority is understood to be supporting, teaching, challenging, holding one another accountable, and caring and mediating for one another and all of God's creation. It is an understanding in which every decision and action is recognized as provisional in virtue of the dynamic quality of the divine-human relation. Thus authorized, we are continually becoming a new creation in covenant.

The one authority, that of God, finds expression within the church in two ways: One is charismatic (persuasive). The other is institutional (conferred by office). Too great an emphasis on the charismatic expression of authority risks losing the truth of the gospel to the most persuasive voice. Too great an emphasis on the institutional expression of authority risks quenching the Spirit.

There were several concerns raised about which we were unable to reach a consensus. They are as follows:

1. There should be teaching offices in the church in order to facilitate the formation of faith. Some persons advocated viewing regional ministers as episcopal officers with teaching authority. However, some expressed concern that an enhanced teaching role for regional ministers not overwhelm the pastoral and administrative aspects of the office. Still others felt that enhancing existing programs and ministries of Christian education would be sufficient. Others advocated the creation of a separate teaching office, in addition to the existing offices of ministry.

2. We should create a process, involving all manifestations of the church (general, regional, and local), by which we arrive at an authoritative confession of faith.

3. We should reclaim the role of ministers as teachers of the faith.

These issues deserve wider consideration in the Christian Church (Disciples of Christ).

Congregational Life and Discipline

The congregation is a community called to witness in word and deed to God's presence in the world for the glory of God. As a Spirit-filled, Spirit-directed, Spirit-empowered community it bears witness to and for the gospel of Jesus Christ for the benefit of the world.

The purpose of congregational life is to glorify God. It is in this sense that worship is rightfully understood as being at the center of congregational life. There are a variety of aspects of congregational life, yet each must find its ground in this most basic purpose. The variety of aspects of congregational life are revealed through scripture, tradition, and contemporary practice.

These aspects include (though it is not an exhaustive list) doing justice, serving the world, incarnating the gospel and fostering solitude, prayer, meditation, and Bible study. Together these aspects of congregational life constitute the practices and habits of the heart and soul through which the congregation disciplines its life and thereby witnesses to the glory of God.*

What Is Congregational Life and Discipline?

It has been suggested that our understanding of congregational discipline include not only the traditional spiritual disciplines but a congregational exercise of asking itself questions (e.g., What practices or disciplines could individuals be involved in that would help them grow in faithfulness? What practices would congregations be involved in for the same purpose?) Christian faith becomes vital within congregations through ordered life together and for others.

This ordered life grows out of who we are as Disciples:

1. We are a biblical people, committed to studying the Scriptures and allowing them to inform our faith.

---

*Several members of our group expressed concern that the word *discipline* may stir up undesired images of authoritarian and judgmental actions, but we have chosen to retain the word in several places in this working paper. We have done so for at least two reasons: first, the word *discipline* occupies an important place in the history of Christian thought about the church; and second, we think that the very complexity of the term forces us to rethink the issues. We mean to suggest that *discipline* refers primarily to the nurturing and ordering of Christian life and not primarily to correction or punishment.

2. We are a spiritual people, seeking the inspiration and the empowerment of the Holy Spirit.

3. We are a reasonable people, bringing the affirmations of faith into dialogue with reason.

4. We are an ecumenical people, committed to our Lord's prayer that all might be one.

5. We are an evangelistic people, witnessing to our faith so that all might believe.

By so living, we grow in faith, do servant ministry, and become more responsible stewards of all that is entrusted to us.

Three Resources Informing Congregational Life and Discipline

Congregational life and discipline are rooted in the theological resources of the Christian Church (Disciples of Christ). Three manifestations of these theological resources that inform our ordered lives are a reappropriation of the Disciples tradition, an exploration into the nature and significance of the covenantal life by which members of our congregations share ministry, and a renewal of the biblical call to repentance and mutual accountability.

1. The Disciples tradition has been rightly described earlier as biblical, spiritual, reasonable, ecumenical, and evangelical. Congregations in our tradition, therefore, acknowledge Scripture as the chief resource in the formation of the character of Christian community and Christian identity. One gift of Disciples congregations is the use of the insight of human mind to appropriate the teachings of Scripture and apply the current context in which congregations live.

   We affirm this collective insight as being guided, chastened, and formed by the action of the Holy Spirit, who is God's animating presence in congregational life.

   Thanks to our tradition, Disciples congregations know and understand themselves as contributing to and being shaped by the vision of the unity of Christ's whole church, and of the ultimate unity of the whole created order, toward which we work and live. Empowered by the transforming grace and judgment of the living God revealed to us in our Lord Jesus Christ, Disciples congregations are impelled to renew and reclaim our call to witness to the whole world the saving love and power of God. Disciples of Christ, as they live ordered lives in congregations, both respond to and proclaim the witness of both Testaments: "You shall love the Lord your God with all your heart, and with all your soul and with all your mind and with all your strength" and "you shall love your neighbor as yourself" (Deuteronomy 6:14; Leviticus 19:18; Mark 12:28-34; Matthew 22:34-40).

2. The congregation is a community of persons who are called by the gospel of Jesus Christ into a covenantal relationship. This relationship exists for the care and nurture of each other in order that each might witness to God in Jesus and minister to human hurts and needs beyond his or her faith community. The congregational covenant is informed by an emergent faith dialogue that leads to Christian formation, commitment, responsibility, and accountability.

This corporate vision calls forth an understanding of how persons have been given gifts by the Holy Spirit so we can function together in a mutually shared ministry among all disciples. The *laos* (the whole people of God) joins together in ordering congregational life in such a way that all Christians find legitimation, recognition, and affirmation to minister on behalf of the congregation. One way in which this takes shape is in offices of leadership—elders, deacons, pastors, department and auxiliary heads. Leaders should be models of self-discipline.

Such persons are called to service as part of their self-understanding and personal identity as Christians. The church seeks to "equip the saints for the work of ministry, for building up the body of Christ, until we all attain to the unity of the faith . . ." (Ephesians 4:12-13). Through study and spiritual renewal the congregants seek to be effective ambassadors for Christ in all arenas of life (e.g., to the boardrooms of the powerful and as waiters at the tables of the poor).

The congregational covenant is governed by an inclusivity that in love embraces diversity—female and male, all races and all classes—in the recognition that each person may have an incarnational and transformational impact upon the world. Hence the evangelical and diaconal ministry is shared by all within the congregation.

3. The congregation, further, is a community of persons who are called to repentance and mutual accountability. We recognize that, in the community of faith, the gospel both confronts and comforts: It confronts us with our sin and unfaithfulness so that we may then hear the comforting news of divine forgiveness and peace. Thus repentance, confession, and the claiming of divine grace become part of the rhythm of congregational life. And as we live by this rhythm, we create a loving atmosphere where we increasingly are enabled to call one another to heed the imperatives of the gospel—the imperatives to be conformed to the image of Christ rather than to the values of the world.

The call to repentance and accountability in a community of love is one of the characteristics that most clearly distinguish the church from the world. It is a process of diagnosis and treatment that is critically important for the healing and health of the body of Christ. Thus we reaffirm the charge of St. Paul to the congregation in Rome: "Do not be conformed to this world but be transformed by the renewal of your mind, that you may prove what is the will of God, what is good and acceptable and perfect" (Romans 12:2). (For related texts, see Ephesians 4:22-23; Hebrews 10:23-25; 1 Peter 1:13-17.)

Evangelism

Desperate for direction in evangelism? Although this paper is essentially a *report* of the working group on evangelism, we hope it is more. We believe it can be a springboard for reflection and discussion of the direction of Disciples evangelism in the 21st Century. Join us in this exploration.

I. Because we believe that the *message* is central and determinative to the task of evangelism, we first turned to the definition of the gospel. We soon learned what we should have known all along: There are many ways the gospel has been and can be expressed and understood. What follows is one way, but one that we believe includes three elements that are essential to any definition.

The gospel is (1) the message of (2) God's forgiving, accepting and renewing love (3) revealed in the life, death, and resurrection of Jesus Christ.

This is a purposefully crisp statement. Any particular proclamation of the gospel must speak to the needs and experiences of the persons to whom it is addressed. Hence, in differing circumstances the evangelist may speak of the forgiveness of sins, of the liberation from the "principalities and powers," of the empowerment of the powerless, of the breaking of the curvature of the self upon the self, of reconciliation with God, of eternal life, etc.

To say this another way, the gospel is entrusted to the church, in the name of Jesus Christ. It has given birth to the church, its steward in the world, and remains the basis for the continuing renewal of both the church and the world.

II. Evangelism is the proclamation of the gospel in word and deed, a communication of the ultimate significance of the Christian faith. Evangelism is the primary, if not the sole, vocation of the church. Evangelism undergirds every aspect of the personal and corporate life of believers.

III. Why do we engage in evangelism? There are many motivations. Chief among them is the conviction that we are loved by God in Christ. The irrepressible power of Jesus' life, death, and resurrection evokes in us the desire to glorify God for that gracious act. Love and concern for our fellow human being is generated, and we seek to share the gospel because it enables others to experience grace, forgiveness, self-acceptance, relationship with God, and abundant life. We affirm that this experience is present now, and, though we differ in our understanding of the consummation of all things, we agree that the gospel gives us lively hope.

IV. *Issues and concerns.* This understanding of the gospel and of evangelism has some specific implications for the 21st Century. Of course much more work needs to be done, but the working group has identified some issues and concerns it believes should be high on the agenda. These may be considered elements of a general strategy for both reflecting on and doing evangelism. That reflection should lead to a clear understanding of the gospel and include a thorough investigation of the universality of sin. In addition the strategy should account for the needs and circumstances of particular groups. It should integrate persons into all aspects of congregational life (e.g., worship, education, counseling, etc.). Indeed this evangelistic strategy may be expected to lead present church members into deeper levels of commitment to the gospel. Finally, such a strategy calls the church to continually reexamine all of its activities and motives in light of the gospel.

Global Mission

Group 1

In faithfulness to the commission of Christ that the gospel be proclaimed throughout the world, we offer ourselves in celebration of God's present activity and in anticipation of the coming reign of God, to whom belongs all power and glory.

Confession

We confess that we have been captives of our own social, economic, and political systems that have kept us from seeing the plight of the whole human family, our sisters and brothers in our midst and around the world. While we have spoken of our commitment to evangelism, we have often acted as if the evangel were only for those already like us and have forgotten that most of the world is hungry, poor, and marginalized. We confess that we have trivialized the gospel, which calls for the radical transformation of persons and the societies in which persons live.

We confess our sectarianism and our unwillingness to find Christ alive and at work among those of diverse religious commitments, color, nationality, economic status, and world view.

We confess that we have defended with violence and the threat of violence our affluence in a hungry world, and that we have not stood in solidarity and partnership with the wretched of the earth—our brothers and sisters by the grace of God.

We confess that we have not celebrated the gifts and the graces God has wrought in Christians in other places and in persons of other faiths.

Affirmation

We affirm that the gospel calls us, together with the whole church of Jesus Christ, to a preferential option for the poor, the voiceless, the nonpersons, and the marginalized, both those in our midst and throughout the world.

We affirm a new commitment to partnership in which we affirm and celebrate the diversity of evidences of God's work and mercy among our brothers and sisters in the world. While affirming the primacy of the revelation that has come to us in the Bible and in the person of Jesus, the Christ, we increasingly find our witness together with other Christians, with other religious bodies, and with all of God's children everywhere, of any or of no religion. We often discover the Christ we know already in their midst under other names, forms, and ceremonies.

We affirm that the church is called to participate in God's present activity and to live in anticipation of the coming reign of God and that we see God's activity among others through: (1) new illumination of the biblical witness, (2) the emergence of new forms of church life (e.g., base Christian communities), (3) liturgical traditions that joyfully express the presence of God, and (4) a spirituality that is not limited to our Western rationality. We affirm that all these signs of the kingdom, which have come to others, are ours to share as we receive the gifts of grace God has already offered our brothers and sisters, and as we offer to the world the gifts and graces that have come to us.

We affirm our need for a spirituality in which we are encountered by the Mystery before which we live and which transcends any human effort to limit the grace of the one who is *holy*. We affirm our need to receive as a gift of God's grace the encounters of the Spirit, which those in other places and at other times have found and known.

Commitment

We commit ourselves to a mission on six continents in which we are both givers and receivers of the gifts and graces of God.

With Alexander Campbell, who based his appeal for reformation on the fact that Christianity is by nature a social religion and hence must be exhibited as well as proclaimed (*Christian Baptist*, 1823: 16), we commit ourselves anew to this principle. We call on other Disciples of Christ to exhibit and proclaim with us our faith by experientially demonstrating through the actions and fellowship of our local congregations and other manifestations of the church our oneness with people of various racial, ethnic, and economic backgrounds. We commit ourselves to a search for a tangible expression of our solidarity with and on behalf of the marginalized and the poor.

We call on the church to allocate time, ability, and funds to the economic, political, and social reordering that moves toward a more just world in which there is equity of power as well as wealth.

We commit ourselves to the continuation of an ecumenical agenda with the whole people of God.

We commit ourselves to a renewal of evangelism among those of us who live amidst the no-longer Christians as well as those we have called the not-yet Christians.

We commit ourselves to an openness to evidences of God's action, even when our privileges and our structures are threatened.

Group 2

Recognition

We as Disciples recognize the biblical and theological basis for global mission as reflected in the Preamble to *The Design for the Christian Church (Disciples of Christ)*.

We recognize that Disciples congregations, particularly the women's organizations in them, give untold hours and millions of dollars to enhance God's global mission.

We recognize that the world is and will continue to be pluralistic in culture and religion. The church is and will be manifest within the multiple cultures of the world. Global mission today, therefore, involves partnership with other Christian communities.

We recognize that, in addition to Christian communities, many others are devoted to one or more specific goals within God's global mission, and that from time to time, we work together with them.

Confession

We confess that we have considered mission "our" gift to the world.

We confess that we have failed to see ourselves as needy.

We confess that we are all too often culturally myopic—and resist efforts of others to correct our vision.

We confess that we resist the judgment of God that others bring to us.

We confess that worshiping idols of consumerism, militarism, nationalism, isolationism, sexism, and racism is in opposition to God's global mission.

Affirmation

We affirm God as the creator of all peoples, who sent Jesus to reconcile us to God and to each other—person to person, sex to sex, race to race, nation to nation, culture to culture.

We affirm that global mission is God's, and we seek to participate in it.

We affirm that some of the unrest in the world that leads to justice and compassion is the fruit of God's global mission.

We affirm our participation in world, regional, national, and local councils of churches.

We affirm that we are called by the gospel to witness in word and action to justice and peace.

We affirm that participation in God's mission demands that we make a preferential option for the poor.

Commitment to Action

We commit ourselves to seek God's agenda in global mission, instead of our or others' agendas.

We commit ourselves to dialogue with people in other cultures and religions even though it is risky and demanding.

We commit ourselves to walk with people of our own and

other cultures in their joys and sorrows, sharing our faith and attending to the sharing of their faith.

We commit ourselves to make, with God's help, the world and our own society more just and to work for a world at peace. To achieve these ends, we encourage more participation in creative programs, such as the Shalom Congregation program.

We commit ourselves to share with others our Christian commitment, giving the credit for any good therefrom to God.

Ministry

Reflecting the convictions and concerns of seventy-eight persons in the working group on ministry, this paper sets forth issues deemed to be of particular importance for the church now as well as in the 21st Century. Many members contributed portions of our statement, with little time for editing and polishing a complete document. We ask wide attention to this paper throughout the Christian Church because of the urgency of the issues raised.

I. Theological Reflection on Ministry

The ministry of the body of Christ, the church, is the calling to proclaim the reign of God and its fulfillment in a broken, sinful, hurting world. This ministry is carried out by a people who have heard the good news of Jesus Christ, who have experienced the grace and redemption of God, who in faith affirm God's claim on their lives. Ministry is not merely local, but worldwide, with apostolic, pastoral, social, and ecumenical dimensions.

Ministry bears responsibility toward two distinct publics who are both local and worldwide: the gathered community of faith and those unaffiliated with it. The witness of Christian ministry seeks the conversion, both of those who are nominally Christian and of those entirely outside the church.

The laity brings a broad spectrum of gifts to ministry. As an ordination into the universal priesthood of believers, baptism unites all Christian people in the calling of the servant church. Week by week the gathering at the table of communion empowers them anew for the shared task. Faithful ministry to the 21st Century will require more creative ways of recognizing and using these gifts of all the baptized for the ministry of Christ. The tensions that arise between clergy and laity indicate the need for clearer recognition of their respective responsibilities and their mutual need of one another in common fulfillment of God's will.

In the spirit of Christ's inclusiveness, women and men, persons of various ethnic and cultural origins, mature persons of all ages, and persons challenged by physical and emotional disabilities, are all appropriate witnesses and representers of the gospel of Christ to the world. The inclusiveness of Christ's gospel requires a concept of wholeness in ministry with openness to all such persons as well as to new dimensions and styles of working. The ordination of women to ministry will deepen and enrich the character of ministry as a whole. Similarly, the unique contributions of racial and ethnic minorities to ministry will enhance its service to all humanity. Christians with physical disabilities also have potential for ministry, which the church can no longer afford to ignore.

II. Ministry to the Future

The 21st Century will bring important advances in science and technology. Through developments in communication the world will become an even smaller and more dangerous place. Therefore, even to speak of the 21st Century is to speak out of Christian hope.

These new advances will make interreligious and Christian ecumenical dialogue increasingly important in an effort to engage the emerging realities of "the world." Such recent developments as *in vitro* fertilization, surrogate motherhood, and life-sustaining medical practices as well as the probable existence of space stations with new potential for good or evil, will call for examination and renewal of ethical systems. This has profound implications for the curricula of our seminaries with an increasing need for interdisciplinary studies.

Individuals will face complex social, economic, and political issues. Needs arising in the gathered community will be at once personal and institutional in character. The needs of persons within the church will mirror the pluralistic reality of humankind, imposing new demands—individual, social, and structural. Global problems of hunger, overpopulation, changing technology. militarism, racism, and interreligious strife crowd the agenda for ministry.

To respond to these needs we will be called back to our roots as a people bearing witness to God's intention for the future and abiding promise to make all things new. Creatively shaping and sharing a ministry that is first of all centered upon Christ as the supreme minister of God's mission to the world, the universal priesthood of believers (the ministry of the *laos*) is the primary form of Christ's ministry today.

Authentic ministry necessarily bears the mark of servant-hood in ministering to those on the Jericho road of human need, the mark of reconciliation in the removal of all that divides and separates people from God and one another, and the mark of solidarity in identification with God's "preferential option for the poor." Such a ministry not only renews our own life as a church, but makes its contribution to the one universal church of God.

Within the context of the ministry of the whole people of God, we see the service of the eldership and of the ordained ministry. We reaffirm the special role of the elder, working in relationship with clergy in equipping and empowering each believer in the body of Christ. In the quest for the mutual recognition of ministers throughout the Christian world, Disciples will persist in intensive ecumenical dialogue and witness.

Effective ministry for the 21st Century will more adequately affirm traditional and nontraditional roles of ministry in order to care for an ever-increasing population of persons with special needs. These include older adults, singles, families in poverty, persons with disabilities, the gifted, the aging, and other exceptional persons of all ages. All these needs lay a claim on the ministry of the church.

The work of ordained ministry rightly takes on a variety of forms including those of pastors, ministers of Christian education, ministers of music, chaplains, pastoral counselors, and others yet to be developed in response to emerging needs. Bivocational and intentional interim ministries are emerging in response to new needs. The prophetic, priestly, rabbinic, and pastoral offices that have characterized ministry from biblical times continue as essential elements in these varied forms of ministry.

III. Sustaining the Ministry

A. *The Order of Ministry*

The Christian Church (Disciples of Christ) in the 21st Century will fulfill its mission and purpose partly through growing understanding of the Order of Ministry as a corporate entity. The ministry of the church is not merely a list of certified individuals. It is a collegial body that gives concrete expression to the concept of "ministers" as members of one another, coworkers in the apostolic tradition, who demonstrate in their life together the unity of the Spirit in the bond of peace. Only in such unity can they be faithful servants of Christ and of his body, the church. The order of ministry will then find collegial expression in all manifestations of the church—local, regional, and general. Ministers together will provide in their collegial life for mutual support, nurture, discipline, biblical and theological reflection, encouragement in continuing education, dialogue, consensus-seeking, and spiritual formation and enrichment, all in responsible relationship with the whole church.

Moreover, a church concerned for the health of its common life will give attention to the welfare of its ordained ministers. We propose certain special needs:

1. the service of a "shepherding bishop" as pastor to those in the Order of Ministry within each region,
2. provision for "career development" and reassessment for those in the Order of Ministry within each region,
3. a General Division of Ministry incorporated into the *Design* to coordinate the services of ministry-related agencies such as the General Board Task Force on the

Ministry, Department of Ministry, Council on Theological Education, Pension Fund, Conference of Regional Ministers and Moderators, regional commissions on the ministry, and other groups relating directly to those in the Order of Ministry.

B. Recruitment, Screening, and Preparation

In the 21st Century the church will necessarily continue to recruit, nurture, and care for those persons who in response to God's call prepare for admission to the Order of Ministry. The church is responsible to help Christians understand the meaning of Christ's commission for their lives and to evaluate their individual ability to serve in particular ways.

The recruiting of persons for ministry has been most effectively done in local churches, at summer conferences, and on college campuses. We call for the church's prayerful attention to the enlistment of its most capable women and men in the work of ministry. Special programs may be needed to focus on the enlistment of women and ethnic minorities.

Those who respond to the call require the care of the church through regional commissions on ministry, with guidance regarding their specific gifts for ministry and their options for preparation and specific types of service. Those not suited for the ordained ministry need assistance in finding appropriate ways to fulfill their Christian calling. Persons from other communions seeking standing within the Order of Ministry will need counsel respecting the church's policies and procedures.

The church through its regions will oversee the education of its ministers in order to prepare pastors, who—by spiritual formation, study in college and seminary, and practical experience—will embody the qualities of the Christian life and perform with skill the arts of ministry. Such preparation will include a responsible knowledge of Disciples tradition, policy, and practice.

C. Ordination and Licensing

We affirm our present policies on ordination and licensing, including the responsibilities assigned to regions,

31

congregations, laypersons, and ordained ministers in the process of ordaining and licensing. It is crucial that laypersons play a substantial and equitable role in the work of the commissions.

D. *Financing, Relocation, and Support Systems*
   1. The church needs to find several models for financial support for those in the Order of Ministry. A large percentage of congregations in the 21st Century may lack the financial resources to maintain a seminary-educated leadership.
   2. We encourage the church to explore procedures for the equitable financing of those accepted into the Order of Ministry.
   3. Just as congregations are encouraged to utilize interim ministries as a creative period in their histories, some persons in the Order of Ministry will be encouraged to undertake this specialized form of service.
   4. We encourage regions and areas to improve the processes for helping ministers seeking to relocate, with attention to finding areas of service for clergy couples. Computers may well be used to facilitate the task.
   5. We urge upon every congregation the development of pastoral relations committees for the intentional, holistic nurturing of those serving in the Order of Ministry and for strengthening the ministry of each community of faith.
   6. While affirming the present relocation system, we call for the church to develop means to care for those whom our structures cannot or will not accomodate: those in transitional crises, those repeatedly neglected by search committees, those who are unjustly terminated or abused by their churches for taking courageous stands, and women and members of ethnic minorities who have been rejected by congregations.

E. *Discipline*
   We call for exploration into means by which the church can pastorally intervene on behalf of congregations whose ministers' actions are destructive to their life; investigation of means by which regions may appro-

priately discipline ministers whose deeds are harmful to the whole church, finding pastoral ways for the regions to address congregations who malign their ministers (or several ministers in succession), the development of a churchwide set of criteria to enable all our regions to operate out of common policies and standards in these matters.

F. *Spiritual Development*

A congregation rightly expects its minister to be constant in deepening her/his spiritual growth and to keep him/herself open to learning experiences across the years of pastoral service. The church will encourage this development through financial support, study leaves, and special events. Prior to any serious framing of a "theology of ministry" is a clear "doctrine of creation" that embraces a theology of self-care. To be a trustee of the created order involves the development of a personal ecology, for which each minister is largely responsible, with its mental, emotional, physical, and spiritual levels. The whole church, in encouraging and sustaining such a process, affirms the doctrine of re-creation. Seminaries can place in juxtaposition the teaching of pastoral care and the care of the pastor and spouse. Supportive collegial relationships may serve as a paradigm of caring love. Inasmuch as the "practice" of ministry drifts typically toward *doing* rather than *being*, the care and feeding of the interior life is pivotal in addressing issues of moment for Disciples ministry.

IV. Conclusion

The working group on ministry offers this paper as an expression of the convictions and concerns of those present for reflection and thought. Serious study of such issues as they relate to ministry in the 21st Century will lead to clearer theological understanding of ministry and a deeper commitment to the mission of the church.

The working group recommends for study and reflection the following existing documents that deal with the issue of ministry:

33

- *The Design of the Christian Church (Disciples of Christ)* "A Word to the Church on Ministry" received at the 1985 General Assembly in Des Moines
- *Baptism, Eucharist and Ministry* (WCC) *COCU Consensus*
- *The Nature of the Church: Ministry Among Disciples*, by Newell Williams
- "Policies and Criteria for the Order of Ministry of the Christian Church (Disciples of Christ)," 1985

The working papers presented to the group by Clark Gilpin, Joyce Basey Coalson, and Robert Welsh contributed substantially to the thinking of the working group and are recommended for study.

Social Transformation

Preface

Unlike the other issues addressed in this conference, social transformation seems to require formal justification. Everyone wants to worship; everyone wants to do ministry and evangelism. Yet, when we make clear the difference between social concern and social transformation, there are significant numbers of people in our congregations who do not think the church should even do social transformation.

Our working group felt compelled to present a theological basis for social transformation and leaves as unfinished the identification of a specific agenda.

We, therefore, offer this consensus document calling the church to do social transformation. We offer it for what it is— only a beginning point. If not followed by action, it is only a collection of words printed on paper.

Report

The Christian Church (Disciples of Christ), in obedience to the Lordship of Christ, historically has been a church committed to living out with faithful consistency a deep and abiding passion to address the needs of the poor and outcast members of society. Social concern has found expression in our history in varying ways, such as: war relief efforts, aid to the needy during the depression, refugee resettlement, congregational social services in the cities, care for orphans and dependent adults, and programs like Reconciliation.

Yet, social concern is not equivalent to social transformation. For some, active social benevolence has led to a new awareness: God's justice (some prefer the word *shalom*) demands not only social service, as important as that work is, but also attention focused upon the social systems that create victims in all strata of society. This awareness raises a very important question: Should the church engage in social transformation?

The members of the working group unanimously answered this question in the affirmative while realizing that our denominational tradition has not, to this point in its history, expressed itself as one mind on this question. Therefore, the task before us is to make credible and urgent the church's responsibility for social transformation, and to do so in a theological and ecumenical way. In doing this, we must say something about the relationship of the world and ourselves to God. At this point, we offer these two statements as a place to start.

1. The beginning place for our reflection must be the recognition that the world is God's. From creation, to the story of redemption, through the culmination of history in the reign of God, the scripture provides witness to this fact (for example, Romans 8:18-25).

   Change is inevitable in our world. Christians are faced with the perplexing questions of how to respond to and initiate change. What should be our criteria for action? Composed of communities located in particular cultures, the church must confess its own tendency toward provincialism. Recognition that the world is God's enables us to move beyond criteria based upon cultural values toward an openness to the moral claims of the powerless as well as the powerful. Faithful engagement with change, therefore, is possible only as we transcend parochial interests. This realization leads us to say a word about the church.

2. The church finds its life in the gospel of Jesus Christ. The gospel proclaims God's love offered freely to each and all and commands God's justice for each and all. We accept this statement of the gospel as the foundation for life in the Christian community and for the expression of Christian life in the

world. It is this good news of God's grace that frees us to live through a vision that is self-transcendent. Such a vision breaks down the walls between communities and leads to both communal and individual relationships reflective of the reign of God. Though this process can be painful, it will lead to a fuller realization of God's will in the world. The gospel calls the church to be and model an alternative to the dominant culture, providing a network of support and empowerment to its own people, and a base from which to bind up the wounds in broader social structures.

When the church ignores the fact of change in the world, it deprives the world of the church's witness of God as the center of value beyond the claims of the personal interests embodied in human structures (political, economic, educational, etc.). We recognize the importance of human structures. Life in community requires the development of structures where a system of shared meaning makes moral choices possible. Yet, the abdication of the church's responsibility to speak and act in the world can only further empower the self interests of human structures to control change in the world. Faithful change does not tend to itself. Therefore, the church must actively seek to influence change that is faithful to the gospel. Such an activity requires the broadest possible inclusion of those affected by the change as well as confronting sin in both its individual and corporate manifestations.

We believe it is important to recognize that the power undergirding the church's engagement in social transformation is rooted in experience of God in creation, community, and solitude. Therefore, we urge the church to renew its commitment to the classical disciplines of prayer and study of scripture and emerging expressions of spirituality. As a people grounded in the experience of God, both in history and present life, and informed by theological reflection upon that experience, the church must offer itself individually and collectively to the world to work courageously toward social transformation.

Structure

Our vision for the 21st Century is the whole church giving

evidence of the reign of God through the proclamation of the gospel to the whole world. We envision a church characterized by:

—vitality
—spirituality
—ecumenicity
—inclusiveness
—collegiality
—integrity

Structure cannot provide such characteristics, but it can serve them.

We affirm the structure of the Christian Church (Disciples of Christ) in the United States and Canada. We view it as a vehicle by which we can become an embodiment of Christ in the world. We recognize the *Design* as a living document and acknowledge the need for a continuing process of renewal and structural reform. This process calls for:

A. Affirmation of the covenantal life embodied in the *Design*. We recognize that life in covenant is in tension with the voluntary association that is part of our history and continuing reality. Yet, our commitment to the gospel and to the true nature of the church calls us to an even more mature understanding of covenantal community in the 21st Century.

B. Intensive biblical and theological education and discussion in all manifestations of the church. We believe that this must take place in order to claim the possibilities of the *Design* and understand the meaning and import of issues such as:

—covenantal community
—discipline
—authority
—collegiality
—inclusiveness
—freedom
—diversity
—lay and ordained ministry
—church universal

Opportunities for theological teaching and dialogue include the following:

—worship and liturgy
—constituted deliberative bodies throughout the church—

General Assembly, General Board, regional assemblies, congregational boards, etc.

One of the theological tasks still to be completed is the definition by each manifestation of its particular mission.

C. Better communication and trust among manifestations of the church, related and recognized organizations, and special constituencies and groups such as the following:

—minority congregations and organizations
—issue-oriented organizations
—colleges, universities, and seminaries
—groups with diverse theological perspectives

Bridging gaps among parts of the church will require increased opportunities for lay discussion and involvement.

D. Improved pastoral care of ministers and empowerment of congregations including the following:

—ministerial relocation process
—attention to small and rural congregations
—close-at-hand care through a possible fourth manifestation (area) and/or a greater number of regions
—continuing education of the clergy

E. Broader involvement in the decision-making process. This will require consideration of such matters as the following:

—resolution process (among other possibilities, items to be considered might include long-term discussion of issues before resolution-drafting and options other than "yes" or "no" votes)
—theological grounding for the study of issues
—adequate time for theological reflection and not just with regard to resolutions
—balance between authority and freedom
—possible recognition of a fourth manifestation (area) close to congregations
—celebration of the prophetic potential of dissenting positions

F. Churchwide planning that incorporates such procedures and features as these:

—initiation and coordination by the General Board
—representation in planning that will assure the widest possible "ownership"
—planning and development of the ministries and work for which they are responsible by thc various manifestations of the church
—provision of a process and structure for planning programs and resources for congregational use

G. Enhanced quality of church leadership through:

—recruiting leadership from among our women and minority constituencies
—developing increased lay leadership
—increasing leadership role of the General Board
—providing leadership education and skills training
—striving to fill all positions with faithfully committed, informed, and competent leaders so that they will warrant the support of the church

H. Balance between centralization and decentralization of authority and programming through:

—concern about the overload of regions to the point that they cannot perform well all tasks assigned and accepted
—concern about the weakening of general units to the point that they are not able to carry out their assigned tasks
—striving for equity in the allocation and distribution of funds among regions, general units, and educational institutions
—realignment of the regions, perhaps with some dividing as well as the uniting of existing regions
—reduction of the physical and emotional distance between congregations and their regions, either by developing a fourth manifestation (areas) or increasing the number of regions for better pastoral care and communication

I. Continued evaluation of structure, especially in the light of theology, but also with consideration of such factors as:

—sociological realities

—management theory
—communication possibilities

In conclusion, we believe that structure is intended to facilitate, not hinder, the reign of God. Therefore, it must always be open—including ecumenically open—to the leading of the Spirit into the future.

Worship

Authentic Christian worship includes the human response to God's gracious presence and action, which draws the worshiper into the transcendent mystery of the past, present, and future activity of God in Christ. Christian worship embraces mystery apprehended through the best in human reason. The worship of God is the central and sustaining act of the church. As we move into the 21st Century, it is vital that our energy be directed to the ongoing renewal of worship. The real question is: Will we be able to make decisions together about what occurs in our liturgical life and develop common understandings of its nature and purpose?

As we move into the 21st Century we affirm

—That Christians come together in community around the Lord's Table. In an effort to remain faithful to the biblical witness, when we as Disciples of Christ worship weekly, we include the breaking of the bread (Acts 2:42). We call to mind afresh the life, death, and resurrection of Jesus Christ. By the receiving of the broken bread and the sharing of the cup of blessing, we participate in the fulness of Christ's sacrifice, the depth of forgiveness, and in the overwhelming hope for the coming reign of God. The radical and gracious love of God for us, which the Lord's Supper embodies and joyfully celebrates, becomes a compelling call "to love one another even as God loves us" (1 John 4:11). The ordained and recognized lay ministries combine to represent the wholeness of the service we offer to God by their roles as mutual celebrants at the Table. We acknowledge our tradition of communion prayer that values simplicity, flexibility, and spontaneity.
—That baptism by immersion, on the basis of a mature decision to follow Christ, is the normative mode within the Christian Church (Disciples of Christ). Baptism includes, in its basic under-

standing, the death of the old life enslaved to sin, burial of a person with Christ, and hope of the new life that springs from God's redemptive power. Baptism is the sacramental covenant that binds us into the body of Christ, the church. We accept those persons who have been baptized in other Christian traditions, avoiding and discouraging the practice of rebaptism.

As we move into the 21st Century we encourage:

1. That worship be understood as sacramental, emphasizing that in worship the mystery of God's transcendent presence and action is experienced.
2. That worship be designed to be inclusive of all persons (gender, race, age, culture, disabilities) and open to a variety of expressions and traditions.
3. That careful attention be given to the language of worship, using living images from Scripture, inclusive of all human experience.
4. That immediate attention be given to questions related to the inclusion at the Lord's Table of children and adults prior to confession of faith and baptism, and of baptized young children prior to their affirmation of baptismal vows. Current practice varies, causing confusion and frustration.
5. That the arts (including visual arts, architecture, music, dance, drama, and film) and liturgical symbols (vestments, paraments, stoles, banners, communion vessels, etc.) be explored and developed more fully as a means of celebrating the wholeness of human experience.
6. That we strive toward transcultural experiences in worship, accepting and celebrating diverse contributions to worship so that our liturgical life is enriched by the encounter with people, traditions, and races outside our own experience of faith.

How do we renew worship so that our life of faith as a church can be strengthened? The following are recommended:

1. Strengthen congregational education in the study of scripture and the liturgy, affirming that the various ministries of the church find their grounding in the Bible and worship life.
2. Aid seminarians and pastors in the development of liturgical skills with emphasis on the various traditions, styles, and resources that nourish the life of the Church Universal.

3. Recover the historical emphasis upon prayer and spiritual formation, helping persons deepen their experience of the presence of God, not only in corporate worship, but also in private devotion.
4. Give guidance to congregations toward the creating of liturgical celebrations for the receiving of new members through confession of faith, baptism, confirmation, and transfer of membership.
5. Provide opportunities for recognizing significant events in the spiritual life of individuals and congregations through the renewal of baptism vows.
6. Urge greater attention to the preparation of all communicants so that they will be more fully prepared to experience the full range of meaning implicit in communion (also called the Eucharist).
7. The use of *The Common Lectionary* in weekly worship as the usual source for scripture readings and as the basis for preaching.

Plenary Discussion of Working Group Reports

April 1, 1987

General Comments

The issue of age needs to be accounted for, especially in the 21st Century as the population grows older. (One response disagreed, saying that inclusiveness was mentioned in the reports. Every group did not need to be mentioned by name.)

* * *

The drastic need for education is evident in all of the reports. The call for more education perhaps needs to be stated even more clearly.

* * *

The eschatalogical tension with which Christians live—our relation to the future—needs to be stated more clearly. This is not just a matter of projecting visible trends. The danger, mystery, vulnerability, and newness of the future must be taken into account in these reports.

* * *

We should affirm the way these reports hold evangelism and ecumenism together. This, itself, is a total aspect of our identity.

* * *

The reports are to be applauded for their sensitivity to the marginalized. The prophetic potential of minority groups is powerful, and not only when they are dissenters.

43

We need another conference that will light up the future needs and concerns of those different from us, one that will not presume that we set standards for the future.

* * *

One concern of the laity has not been adequately dealt with: Our historical relationship and current response to the conservative evangelical movement. More attention needs to be given to why they are growing and Disciples are not.

* * *

We need to recognize the tensions between the values of culture and the values of God. Transformation needs to be taken more seriously.

Comments on Particular Group Reports

Evangelism: More attention should be given to the education of children. We need support groups aimed at helping Sunday school teachers. We are losing the children of our members.

Ministry: Clergy couples should be mentioned and attention given to support systems for them.

Authority: The report concludes on weakness rather than strengths. Reorder the wording to read "we are fallible . . . nevertheless courageously . . . ." The report is also still vague on our own identity as Disciples.

Social Transformation: We need pastoral strategies for necessary change. This was not addressed.

Global Mission: We need to think more about what it means practically to speak of a preferential option for the poor.

Worship: Disciples need a resource for liturgical renewal. (A response pointed to the book *Thankful Praise: A Resource for Christian Worship*, just published by Christian Board of Publication.)

Congregational Life and Discipline: We as "Disciples" should affirm the report's emphasis on "discipline."

Joe R. Jones
President, Phillips University
Enid, Oklahoma

Earthen Ambassadors

2 Corinthians 4:1-10; 5:16-21

It is my pleasure and honor to have this opportunity to address this highly anticipated conference. We should all agree that this conference is timely. Certainly the Christian Church (Disciples of Christ) finds itself in a difficult, dismaying, and perhaps even decaying situation. While our numbers steadily dwindle, so too our attitudes give way to despair, confusion, and a lack of confidence in our basic mission. If this conference can be the occasion for a new grasp of our calling and mission, a quickening of the spirit, then it will have done a magnificent service to our denomination and to the universal church.

At the beginning of this sermon let me acknowledge that I preach with one design: to allow us to vividly recapture our calling in the gospel of Jesus Christ and to have the appropriate boldness to proclaim that gospel to the world. I have no new inventions or slick panaceas to commend this day.

It is especially appropriate that we begin by allowing Holy Scripture to convey its witness to us. Hear these striking utterances from the readings for today: "Having this ministry by the mercy of God, we do not lose heart." "By the open statement of the truth we would commend ourselves to every man's conscience in the sight of God." "What we preach is not ourselves, but Jesus Christ as Lord, with ourselves as your servants for Jesus' sake." "We have this treasure in earthen vessels, to show that the transcendent power belongs to God and not to us." "We are . . . perplexed but not driven to despair." "We regard no one from a human point of view." "If anyone is in Christ, he is a new creation." "All this is from God, who through Christ reconciled us to himself and gave us the ministry of reconciliation." "God was in Christ reconciling the world to himself, not counting their tres-

45

passes against them, and entrusting to us the message of reconciliation." "So we are ambassadors for Christ, God making his appeal through us."

In hearing these powerful words, is it not confirmed once again, with freshness and urgency, that God speaks to us through Holy Scripture?

To the end of elucidating this scripture from St. Paul and discerning its light for the church today, I dare to propose a definition of the church around which we can order our thoughts. I suggest to you that "the church is that community of persons called into being by the gospel of Jesus Christ to witness in word and deed to the living God for the benefit of the world." Consider this a doctrinal schema for the interpretation of Holy Scripture.

The first point I want to emphasize from this definition is that the church is a "called" community. The church does not call itself into existence; the church does not give itself its own marching orders; the church is not a democratically self-justifying community. The church is called into existence by the gospel of Jesus Christ. The church exists because something dramatic and revelatory has happened in the life, death, and resurrection of Jesus Christ. When the church loses this sense of being called, then it deteriorates into a disjointed collection of people, stumbling along the paths of self-justification, despair, or quietly acknowledged relativism. At the beginning of the church is the acknowledgement of the good news of what God has done in Christ Jesus, such that the church can no longer regard anyone from a human point of view.

The church has been given one comprehensive and essential task: *to witness* in word and deed to the living God for the benefit of the world. However warm may be our fellowship, however comfortable our gatherings, if we are not a community engaged in witness, then quite simply we are not the church of Jesus Christ. There is no blunter way to put it. The Scripture tells us that we have this ministry by the mercy of God in order that we might provide an open statement of the truth as ambassadors for Christ. A failure to recover this vital and dynamic sense of witness as the mission of the church will guarantee continued futility, despair, and hand-wringing.

Yet we have this treasure—this gospel of Jesus Christ—in earthen vessels, and this needs to be put alongside of "What we preach is not ourselves but Jesus Christ as Lord." In a profoundly important way we must continually hold in tension that we are called to give witness by the very self-disclosure of God and to have a humility that is appropriate to the situation of a limited recipient. And yet, to understand clearly that the church does not preach itself, the church does not proclaim itself, the church is not the message. There is no room for a martial triumphalism of the church. The transcendent power belongs to God, not to us.

We are called to be earthen ambassadors, as I would put it. We are frail, finite, and often prone to mistake and error. No doubt the earthenness of our condition often leads to perplexity and confusion. We would like to be Promethean triumphalists. But we are not. We are ambassadors but of the earthen variety. We are servants who are given a mission that is good news to the world.

As we ponder this earthen witness, let us remember that my definition firmly underscores that it is a witness in *word* and *deed*. The good news must become articulate language that resonates with power and truth. Yet, separated from enactment, separated from deed, the words become vain and empty. I would hope that one of the linch pins of this conference is that we learn to talk about real, passionate evangelization and earnest concern for social justice as two sides of one coin. We shall remain confused and muddled if we think of these as competing missions of the church.

My definition goes on to suggest that we are witness *to the living God*. Here we arrive at the crucial juncture in our reflection. The gospel of Jesus Christ emboldens us to think we have a truthful disclosure of the ultimate source of all things, the Alpha and Omega, the Creator and the Redeemer. This is not a passing insight; this is not mere metaphysical speculation. This is a witness to the living God. This is a witness that God was in Christ reconciling the world to God's self, not counting their trespasses against them. We Christians dare to believe that this disclosure is radical good news: that God's judgment—the only real and ultimate judgment—is the judgment of reconciling love. The God to whom we witness does not ultimately forsake the world, does not reject the world. All persons are at the ultimate source embraced by an unfathomable love. Whatever time and circumstance of history may reject or cast upon its dung heap, God does not.

47

Certainly there are victims of historical forces, but these historical powers do not have the final power to assess the meaning and destiny of these victims, which is the power of final judgment. Only God has that power, and it is the power of redemptive love.

This is not the comfort of "I'm OK" shouted in a loud voice. This is a declaration about how God is disposed toward humankind. Obviously as we meditate on this profoundly deep disclosure we move in the direction of God's universal redemption. Is this not a mystery that is joy and happiness to all people?

I want to rush on and say that this is unmitigated good news that we have to share with the world, but a conversation several years ago with T. J. Liggett reminds me that there is also some relatively bad news. It is not the bad news that God might really change God's mind and reject the naughty children. But it is the relatively bad news to those that truly hear, that now having heard they must change their lives. To hear this gospel is also to hear the firm imperative of a new life, a new creation. Give up the old way of regarding yourself and the world; give up the human point of view; now live freely and liberated in the gospel of Jesus Christ.

Yes, people will hear the witness to this gospel in waves of indifference, open hostility, or faithful response. But even the indifference or the rejection does not alter the ultimate good news about the reality of God's love. It is this living truth that we must return to again and again and speak with imagination, live with creativity, and enact with discipline if we are to be true witnesses to the gospel of Jesus Christ.

We witness for the *benefit of the world*. This contemporary world of ours with all of its warts, its malice, its hatefulness, its ugliness, its pain and suffering, is the world that God loves with an infinite compassionate love. God loves the world not on its own terms but on God's terms. The world's terms and conditions have no ultimate standing. But as we witness to the world we realize that the church, this community of persons called to witness, is not an end in itself. The church aims at the world, the real object of God's love. It has always been a distortion of the gospel to say that the primary object of God's love is the Christian community.

Having now worked through this definition, let me admit that it is finally incomplete. Properly it should say that we are called to witness in word and deed to the living God for the benefit of the world *to the glory of God*. God's life embraces the world and gives it the only real standing it can possibly and ultimately have. But to say this is to acknowledge that God is Alpha and Omega, the beginning and end of all things. The only proper way of grasping this is to acknowledge that God's glory stands at the end of all things. Practically speaking, the church is being called to witness as an earthen ambassador to the world for the glory of God. Thanks be to God that God's ultimate glory includes God's love and redemption of creation.

I hope we hear that the road to recovery and confidence is a road that leads to a new sense of calling by the gospel of Jesus Christ, a new sense of witness in word and deed, a vivid grasp of the reality of God and God's relation to the world. I commend to you a strong sense of the confessional priority of our being called by the gospel of Jesus Christ. Here we are firmly grounded in revelation. I commend a witness that is bold theologically, that does not fear such thinking, but knows that it is inescapable if there is to be a lively witness to God. Let us have a muscular theological zest and courage!

This conference, I pray, will know that God has spoken to us in Christ Jesus. We will know that we are recipients of a calling that is wide and bright, but we will know that we are also earthen vessels. We are not the gospel; the church is but a parable of the kingdom.

Can we not recapture this? Can we not rediscover a mission that is courageous and demanding and uplifting? Can we confess our earthiness and yet be bold without arrogance? Can we be servants of the glory of God?

All this, dear friends, I have dared to preach only in the name of the Creator, the Redeemer, and the Holy Spirit. Amen.

James O. Duke
Professor of Church History
Pacific School of Religion
Berkeley, California

Called By the Gospel That Casts Out Fear

In memoriam, Daniel B. Cobb

The turning of a century is no ordinary time. How could it be? Here ordinary time takes a turn, and if it turns, it can only be for better or for worse. That makes the turning of a century a time of dreams, reveries born of hope and nightmares born of fear. So it was for Disciples a hundred years ago today. Born of their hope were reveries of a Christian century to come. That century, and with it that hope as well, now passes us by, and we gather together to confer about the future. What dreams do we have to share?

Nightmares are perhaps more likely than reveries. That's a sign of our times. Ours is a strife-torn, dangerous world. It is taking its toll on us. Operating alone or in social packs, we grow wary of one another—anxious, resentful, polarized. Fear turns our relationships into rivalries; our business pursuits, into so many protection rackets: our recreation, into escapism. We are, quite frankly, scaring one another to death, and at this rate we may well finish the job before the 20th Century turns.

But beware of voices of doom and gloom. I am the first to raise specters of fear at this conference. God willing, may I be the last one as well. At a time like this, the church that wants to ready itself for the future has to key in on the gospel that casts out fear. Otherwise it will fall short of its Christian calling. Thus the one issue that I put before us—the issue that opens up a long list of others—is this: Shall the church discern its true calling?

This issue will face the church of the future. Of this even a backward-looking church historian can be sure, for it is always so. To be the church is to be about a God-given calling. The church lives—if life there be—outside of itself. A vital power gives it birth, animates it, and empowers its ministry. Hence Christians

50

should think first of what their calling is, and once they think they have it figured out, they should think again.

Our first thought is displayed, for all to see, in how our church chooses to minister to the real world—our worship, our nurture, our solicitude; our moral behavior, our outreach, our social-political involvements; our relationships internal and external. In this realm, call it practice or praxis as you please, the church tips off the world to its sense of calling. As God is our witness, what our church says is telling; its actions speak louder than words; its complacency screams to high heaven.

To be sure, what you see may be all you get. The church's calling is God-given; its sense of that calling is human, often all too human. Not all that the church is and says and does can be passed off as the will of God. Its ministry may be timid, misguided, even counterfeit. Thus conscience requires Christians to give second thought to their sense of calling. This takes reflective thinking, critical, and even self-critical thinking. Let's call it, for the lack of a better term, *theological reflection*. Its place is not in the scholar's study alone. It belongs at every level of church life. It is carried on through study, prayer, dialogue, and debate.

Theological reflection is a sorry substitute for living faith. But it has its value. It can aid that faith by alerting Christians to the temptation to confuse God's good news with messages of our own human making.

This temptation is always near at hand and disguised as an angel of light. Messages of our own making are packaged for popular consumption. They appeal to those of us who make them and those who, like us, stand to benefit from them. Others, of course, get left out. But that seems only proper, considering that the point of such messages is to secure the claims of some against those of others. The bottom line is always the same: God, it is said, belongs to us. The theological problem here is classic; the words are all right, but the order is all wrong.

The gospel is not that God belongs to us, but that we belong to God. It empowers us to confess that we are God's, in life and in death. That's why God's good news casts out fear. And who is this *we*? Not we Disciples or even we Christians, but we the human family—one and all. This is the we who belong not to ourselves but to God.

Messages of fear that parade around as gospel are commonplace. Take, for example, resurgent traditionalism. Here the fear of loss leads to a ministry devoted to self-defense. Under the banner of security, the comforts of the familiar are offered to traumatized souls. Authoritarian, legalistic, exclusivistic—more recently entertaining and activist as well—this version of Christianity confuses the will of God with the preservation of some status quo, be it real or imagined.

Or take, for example, rampant traditionlessness. Here the fear of loss leads to a ministry of self-indulgence. Under the banner of autonomy, the delights of cost-free grace are promoted. Undemanding, faddish, privatistic—this version of Christianity confuses the will of God with whatever satisfies each momentary longing.

Much of the church, and all that was once called mainline Protestantism, is caught in a squeeze play between these two forces. There are still Christians who sense that the church is called to a ministry beyond self-defense and self-indulgence. But they suffer a crisis of confidence. Too conservative for some, too radical for others, they find themselves increasingly marginalized and left to haggle over what it all means. The haggling does nothing to improve their lot. The century ahead looms as their time of trial. Quite naturally, many will say that the church needs to recover its confidence. But the confidence it recovers must be of a very special sort. Hence I would prefer to argue that the church is in need of reminders that real confidence comes only from the gospel that casts out fear.

To the worldwide church in need of such reminders, the Disciples have something to contribute, more perhaps than we commonly admit. Christian humility counsels us to speak modestly of our journey in faith. Nevertheless, it has brought us some insights about discerning the gospel. These insights are truly, if not uniquely, our own. I propose that we look at these insights—and not points of doctrine or forms of worship or church programs—as our gifts to the 21st Century church. Let me mention only a few.

The first is that the gospel cannot be bound. God's good news is greater than the earthen vessels in which we try to contain it. This insight prompted the founders of our church to break with the 19th Century religious establishment. In the name of Christ Jesus, they took issue with creeds and theologies and polities and disciplines and customs—with anything and everything—that hindered access to the gospel. The result was a massive ecclesiastical housecleaning. Less can be more. Christians can show that God's good news is greater than our earthen vessels by showing those vessels no mercy.

Granted, this tactic has its limits. Foremost among them is the tendency to slip from simplicity to oversimplification. But at these limits our founding insight freed Disciples to take another tack. Christians can show that God's good news is greater than our earthen vessels by casting and recasting those vessels with reformist zeal. Flexible, pragmatic, at times experimental—Disciples first proliferated their ministries and then reordered them into a covenantal church.

With this insight comes a Christian commitment at home with critical and even self-critical thinking. Faith is not the end but the beginning of serious questioning. The gospel can withstand such testing; everything else richly deserves it. The upshot is not that Christians can believe whatever they like. It is that they are free to hear the claim of God's good news ever anew. Tolerant, diverse, inquiring—Disciples seek to model a community of faith that discerns its calling through a mutual exchange of ideas, all subject to critical second thoughts.

This sort of free-wheeling gospel freedom has its drawbacks, of course. Many, it seems, take opposition to traditionalism to be an invitation to traditionlessness. And it would be, were it not for a second insight closely linked to the first. It is that God's good news calls forth community. Because we belong to God, we belong to one another. The love of God in Jesus Christ forms us into a community of faith, and this community is called to be an agent of reconciliation in a strife-torn world.

As a community of faith the church needs signs and seals of unity and continuity. Through scripture, the church refreshes its memory of God's historic initiatives; through baptism and the Lord's Supper, it encounters the very touch of God's grace; through its confession of faith, it finds itself giving itself to the crucified one whom God has vindicated. These ties are not to be broken. Nor are they to be taken for granted. They are so familiar that it is easy to forget their fundamental meaning. Amidst despair—despair caused by evil, oppression, poverty, illness, and death—they proclaim the universality and trustworthiness of God's love.

Rightly understood, these signs and seals also keep before the church its calling to reach out in service to others, be they near or far. As God reaches out reconciling the world through Jesus Christ, so the community of faith is to make manifest to the world God's good news. Because of that call, Christians are constrained by joy to invite others to share life together in the community of faith.

This invitation has come to be termed *evangelism*. That's fine, though the term needs clear definition. Evangelism is at root neither a program nor a promotional campaign; it is an act of sharing life in the gospel that casts out fear. Unless and until it keeps in view this life to be shared, the church need hardly be a bother—to God or to others—with its evangelistic claims. But if the church discerns its calling rightly, the impulse to share—to be evangelistic—will be irrepressible. No less irrepressible will be the work of mutual edification, of nurture, and upbuilding the community to its full stature in Christ.

To fulfill its calling, the community of faith is also to be an agent of reconciliation in the wider world. This type of service has come to be termed *mission*. And that too is fine, so long as the meaning of the word is clear. Because God's good news casts out fear, Christians are free to give of themselves for the sake of others. Their efforts, individual and corporate, will be many and varied: to comfort those who are distressed, to feed those who are hungry, to bind the wounds of this world's casualties. And more. They are free to address not merely the results of evil but the structures that perpetuate it. They are free to press for peace, justice, equality, and for new orders of relationship in the social, political, and economic realms.

The gospel creates community, and that community of faith is an agent of reconciliation—this was a hard-won insight for Disciples, and long in maturing. The process should therefore be all the more instructive to us. At its origins our movement spoke of the church as the inbreaking of God's reign on earth. Anti-creedalism notwithstanding, Disciples confessed their faith; anti-sacramentalism notwithstanding, they came to baptism and weekly communion to be touched by God's grace. They rediscovered that the local church was nonetheless church even though it was local.

Over the years that have followed, they learned that to be agents of reconciliation would require more, not less, than vitality in the local congregation. Cooperation, partnership, joint enterprise, and eventually Restructure were necessary. The practical impact of this lesson on our life has already been massive. More massive still is its theological impact. With Restructure, Disciples acknowledge the churchliness of their Christian ministry as a whole. We have not yet fully fathomed the meaning of that agreement. Our life history, however, suggests this. Unity amidst diversity commends covenantal, not hierarchical, relations, and the test of covenant faithfulness is not prooftexting but empowerment for service.

Likewise, the gospel that casts out fear frees Christians to engage in the struggle for peace, justice, and equality. It frees them as well to support those throughout the world who, long oppressed, press their rightful claims to freedom and dignity. By its very nature reconciliation in this sense will be controversial. The church need not—it dare not—shy away from the controversy, so long as it is free of ideology, pressing to make clear to all that its mandate is theological in character. The Disciples are in a position to help keep this mandate before the 21st Century church. But the task of making clear the theological character of that mandate, and then carrying it out through effective action— that will take the wisdom of Christians around the globe.

So it is that the calling of the church is an ecumenical venture. And here is the third insight into the gospel that casts out fear. Our own quest for the unity of the church began at the very moment of our birth. God has never left us without witnesses to the cause. Despite schism and despite complacency, Disciples have never been able to deny the force of Jesus' prayer, "that they may be one."

We do a disservice—to our own tradition, and to the worldwide church of the 21st Century—if we deny the force of Jesus' prayer for unity as we give thought to our "distinctiveness" or our "unique identity." It is one thing for other churches—whatever they may be—to return to yesteryear in search of their identity. It is quite another for Disciples. For what seems to be most distinctive in our history are stinging rebukes of denominational distinctiveness. "Unity is our polar star"; "We will, that this body die, be dissolved, and sink into the Body of Christ at large"; division is "the scandal of Christianity"—what are we Disciples to make of these well-known phrases? We might well look upon them as our gifts to the church of the future.

Fearful of loss, some churches are newly inclined to traditionalism, others to traditionlessness. With insight into the gospel that casts out fear, Disciples may well remind the church, once again, that its future lies in unity, a unity more deep and broad and visible than the world has yet seen. Oneness in Christ is given; reconciliation one with another is yet to be achieved.

The 20th Century has known striking ecumenical advances. But what has been gained may easily be lost, and given its limits, it is a mere shadow of full unity, one with another, in Christ. Ecumenical goodwill too often conceals a "live and let live" attitude that falls short of genuine mutuality. Ecumenical cooperation too often conceals a tactical calculation that falls short of genuine giving and receiving.

If the choice comes down to goodwill or animosity, cooperation or ruthless competition, let us by all means opt for goodwill and cooperation. But our insight into the gospel that casts out fear leads Disciples to press for more. The more is not uniformity. It is instead a mutual relatedness that assures that Christians will face the task of discerning the Christian calling of the 21st Century church together. If they are to understand what it means to be the community of faith and what it means to undertake acts of reconcilation in the world, Christians need one another.

Julia Marie Brown
Vice President, Division of Overseas Ministries
Christian Church (Disciples of Christ)
Indianapolis, Indiana

Issues Confronting the 21st Century Church:

What Can Disciples Contribute?

I have always been a dreamer and what some may consider an oversensitive person; sensitive to the struggles of my church, family, friends, this nation and what it represents, as well as issues related to the global community. As a child growing up in Yazoo, Mississippi, I loved to swing in the homemade swing that my older brothers made by throwing a rope across the limb of a large pecan tree and using a plain board as a seat. I used swinging to daydream and as an escape from the horrible reality of being black in the state of Mississippi. I dreamed about the future that one day I would claim. Never, and I repeat never, did I imagine myself addressing such an auspicious audience on any subject. Here I stand with the guidance of the Holy Spirit to address you on issues confronting the church in the 21st Century and what should be the Christian Church (Disciples of Christ) response. This is indeed a humbling experience.

We could all benefit from our church partners in Africa, Asia, Europe, Latin America, the Caribbean, and the Middle East addressing this conference on the issues that they perceive will confront the church in the 21st Century. It is unthinkable to address these issues without some understanding of issues that will affect the universal church. The division of the world into nation-states does not separate, neither isolate, humanity from humanity. We need to be aware that the peaceful dreams of Christians in the United States may very well represent nightmares for our brothers and sisters globally. We need always to be sensitive to where we stand in relationship to the rest of God's creation.

However, my task is to dream, to look at those issues I perceive will be the challenges of the 21st Century and the opportunities of ministry that will result from these challenges. The most marvelous aspect of this presentation is that it is not written in concrete. I will only point to that which I think is becoming,

57

realizing that we are a people in process. We have the power to make a difference in God's world. I would like for you to listen to this address with this underlying question in the back of your mind, "How can I make a difference in the legacy that I have willingly or unwillingly bequeathed to the children of the 21st Century?"

Allow me to address the issue question. When one is given a once-in-a-lifetime opportunity to participate in a visioning process such as this, one is tempted to highlight issue after issue. However, I have chosen those issues that I think will have a profound effect on life and relationships as we know them today.

There is one critical theological issue that will confront the church in the 21st Century; It will give birth and substance to a number of related issues. It will not be a new phemomenon, rather a growing one, which is the sin of self-interest or plain selfishness from an individual, as well as a collective perspective. William Ramsey put it this way in his book *Four Modern Prophets*: "There are sinful structures, economic systems and political patterns. Sinful as these are, however, they rest upon the selfishness in the human heart."[1]

We Christians living in the United States are victims of a dichotomy. On the one hand, we confess a faith in God, creator of the universe, and in the covenant of love that binds us to God and one another; and on the other hand, we live in a society which promotes the individual over the community. The Christian faith instructs us in an unselfish love, which is described in 1 John 4:7: "Beloved, let us love one another; for love is of God and he who loves is born of God and knows God" (1 John 4:7).

Yet, we have also been indoctrinated into the idea of rugged individualism, and the American dream. We hold in the highest admiration those who have succeeded in obtaining material success. This idea has been spelled out in *Habits of the Heart*, a book on individualism and commitment in American life:

> The American dream is often a very private dream of being the star, the uniquely successful and admirable one, the one who stands out from the crowd of ordinary folk who don't know how, and since we have believed in that dream for a long time and worked very hard for it to come true, it is hard for us to give it up; even though it contradicts another dream that we have, that of living in a society that would really be worth living in.[2]

As a result of our selfishness, we have created a world filled with inhumanity and we have become idolatrous in the process, as we voluntarily give our allegiance to our personal and collective self-interest, while ignoring the desperate cries for liberation that come from people and creation. John MacQuarrie in his book *Principles of Christian Theology* makes this point quite clear when he states:

> Self-idolatry leads into those sins of pride, and so of division, which constitute one form of existential imbalance. On the other side, idolizing of things leads into the sins of indulgence and greed. Again this is typical of the technological era, when the multiplication of devices has in turn multiplied artificial needs and appetites. . . . sins of pride and indulgence can and usually do go together and this is easily intelligible in the light of their common origin in idolatry.[3]

In the midst of our sins, we are often driven to despair, therefore, it is important to highlight that, for a Christian, the future is always a time of opportunity and hope. Jurgen Moltman puts it best in his book *The Theology of Hope*, when he states, "This hope makes the Christian church a constant disturbance in human society. . . . It makes the church the source of continual new impulse toward the realization of righteousness, freedom and humanity in the light of the promised future that is to come."[4] This understanding of hope will mean a loss for us, a death to our selfishness. It is a hope that God will melt us and allow us to be formed again. This hope implies a conversion from our self-centeredness and greed to another way of being in the world, which is grounded in our love of God and humanity.

The sin of self-interest, which leads to self-idolatry, breeds issues such as economic oppression, militarism, racism, and sexism. This is by no means an exhaustive list, however, these are the issues that I have chosen to highlight this evening. It is my belief that all of these issues relate to the sin of self-interest or self-idolatry.

First, let's examine what I perceive to be the most critical issue that results from this sin. It is the growing unequal distribution of resources within nations and between "developed" and "developing" nations, in other words economic oppression.

It is estimated that, excluding China, 750 million persons live in absolute poverty in developing countries, which does not take into account the millions of people starving in developed countries, such as the United States. Almost half of these victims are children. As a result, the United Nations Children's Fund reports that 40,000 small children die from malnutrition and infection daily. Arthur Simon reports in *Bread for the World* that:

> The world is presently adding 82 million persons each year to its number, the equivalent of the entire U.S. population every three years. Most of the growth is taking place in poor countries among poor people. Today these countries already contain more than three-fourths of the earth's population. By the turn of the century they will account for more than four-fifths of the human race. All the while demand for the world's food supply will climb sharply each year, and barring unprecedented global efforts increasing numbers will end up in the hungry categories.[5]

Add to an already desperate situation the impact of the third world debt, which in 1984 was estimated at $895 billion, and what you get are the open wounds of Christ. This debt does not only impact the present, but it robs the children of these developing countries of any real chance for a future.

The experience of the Division of Overseas Ministries of the Christian Church (Disciples of Christ) reveals that poverty manifests itself in third world countries in various degrees. There is even a degree of human misery that could be described as "beyond poverty," a degree in which human beings are no longer living like garbage, but have actually become garbage; a degree of human deterioration in which the possibilities of repair are uncertain, despite any available resources.

We need to understand that the present economic imbalance experienced by third world countries is the result of an exploitative and oppressive system that places the self-interest of the privileged and wealthy above that of the poor and oppressed. As followers of Jesus, we are required to walk with and be committed to the poor. The 21st Century will require us to go beyond cosmetic charity to a more equitable sharing of the world's resources.

Second, we must look at another life-threatening issue, militarism. The church's concern is world peace, and militarization is a deterrent of world peace. The church finds itself at a unique point in history with the advent of the nuclear age that brings with it the power to ultimately bring life, as we know it, to an end. The issue is, how can the church preserve life in such a world? According to John 10:10-11, Jesus stated, "The thief comes only to steal and kill and destroy: I come that you may have life, and have it abundantly. I am the good shepherd. The good shepherd lays down his life for the sheep."

What does it mean for the church to be the good shepherd at a time when increased military spending is the order of the day? According to Lee Hamilton, Indiana Congressman from the ninth district, President Reagan submitted a budget for 1988 that exceeded $1 trillion. The largest area of federal spending is defense, which is projected at $298 billion. The biggest defense increase will be for the Strategic Defense Initiative, while at the same time the budget is reduced as it relates to programs that help the disadvantaged and the poor. This type of unbalanced spending is not only peculiar to the United States, but is beginning to become a worldwide phenomenon, as both the developed and developing nations seek to protect what they perceive to be in their self-interest. The ironic result of this irrational thinking is that the very defense, as it is called, that we are stockpiling in order to protect our self-interest has the capacity to destroy life in all of its forms.

If it is indeed the church's role to preserve life, and the church recognizes that in order to preserve life it is critical to maintain world peace, the church must realize that world peace will never exist where people are hungry, homeless, and exploited. We understand that unless we are willing to contribute to solving the problems of the landless, homeless, illiterate—social injustice in any form—world peace will not become a reality.

Third, I submit that racism is also linked to a sense of self-interest. Racism denies the image of God, which exists within all persons, regardless of race. Therefore, it is understood as sin. There is a tendency for some people to need to feel superior to others in order to give them status and to elevate their sense of self. Racism reflects self-interest on a collective level. It inflicts a heavy toll on those who practice it, those who tolerate it, and especially those who suffer from it.

Former President Jimmy Carter recently spoke at Rice Institute for Policy Analysis in Texas. He said he recalled when the television screens were filled with little Ethiopian children walking along with distended bellies and dying in the arms of their dying mothers. He said, "It's hard for me to believe those children in the eyes of God, are as important as Amy . . . . How many of these black kids does it take to equal one Amy? Fifteen? Twenty? Ten? Five?" He concluded, "I think the answer is one. But it's hard for me to believe this."[6] I assume Jimmy Carter was attempting to explain how racism is inherently present in white America.

We assume that racism is a dead issue or simply past history. However, violent racism is on the rise globally; bear with me as I speak to the escalation that is occurring in the United States. *The Monitor*, a publication of the Center for Democratic Renewal, reported that in January 1986, a known klansman and six others, armed with baseball bats, threatened and assaulted a group of Hispanics at a Cedartown, Georgia, bowling alley. Their main target was Carlos Guzman, 16 years old, for "dating white girls." On March 23, 1986, Philadelphia, Pennsylvania, four whites were charged with intimidation and terrorist threats for allegedly making racial slurs and throwing rocks at the home of an Asian family in a predominately white neighborhood. On December 20, 1986, in New York City, a black man was killed when a mob of young whites chased him onto a busy thoroughfare in the predominantly white neighborhood of Howard Beach.[7]

Racism is not just peculiar to the United States; it is indeed a global problem. Little has been said regarding the cruel racist government of South Africa. The blood of black Africans—men, women, and children—constantly flows in South Africa. We know that in the end the sheer numbers of the black population will insure that South Africa will eventually be governed by blacks. Why does blood have to be shed and people brutally killed when those victims who suffer the evil of racism begin to say "no more"? It is because the god of self-idolatry demands our ultimate allegiance; that is why it is so difficult to give up. People tend to protect their ungodly self-interest even at the expense of death.

Fourth, sexism is another significant issue that the church will face in the 21st Century. Women globally are victims of sexism, regardless of class, cultural, or racial differences. However, different types of exploitation are seen in various cultural settings. Sexism promotes the self-interest of men over women; it therefore places men in a privileged position and promotes a patriarchal world view. This is apparent in the church as well as in the secular world.

Some will say we need to hear afresh the status of women in the world today, and their pain as they labor under the most humiliating conditions in which human beings find themselves; but I say we already know this. My question is: What will the church of the 21st Century do about it? For example, the office on Global Education of Church World Service reports that:

> In the Third World, where three-fourths of the world's people live, rural women account for more than half of the food produced. Women are the sole breadwinners in one-fourth to one-third of the families in the world. The number of women-headed families is rapidly increasing. So far earnings differentials persist even at equivalent levels of training. As a rule, women work longer hours than men. Many carry triple work loads in their households, labor force, and reproductive role. Rural women often average an 18-hour day. Nutritional anemia is a serious health problem for women in the Third World. In so called First World countries, relatively few women have entered occupations traditionally dominated by men. Most women remain highly segregated in low paying jobs.[8]

Of the one million people who die annually of hunger-related causes and the one billion that endure chronic undernourishment and other poverty deprivations, the majority are women and children. Although women suffer from oppression and exploitation at a disproportionate level relative to men, they are rarely consulted about possible solutions because government and international bodies that discuss the world's problems are almost exclusively male.

Sexism is also prevalent within the church. Women generally are not encouraged to enter the ministry and are at best tolerated when they insist God called them to preach (this is especially true of black female clergy). However, female students in our seminaries range from 30-40 percent of the total student population. These women have something to contribute to the whole church. We must not allow them to be underutilized! However, women are usually relegated to assistant pastor or appointed to small churches that men don't want to serve. Women involved with religious institutions must take on responsibilities often not accepted by men. Although women comprise more than 50 percent of the church's membership, they are by no means at the higher levels of decision-making in the church. Am I serious? Just take a look at the regional ministers and general unit presidents of the Christian Church (Disciples of Christ).

Women have begun to respond to the social, political, and economic realities of their lives. Feminism has provided a theory that clarifies the nature of women's experiences, and makes possible positive changes that would eliminate not only sexist exploitation but racism and oppression as well.

As an activist and a member of a marginalized community within the United States, I must confess that it would be easy for me personally not to feel any responsibilities for the unequal distribution of the world's resources and other injustices that exist globally. As long as I consider myself marginalized, having been born poor, black, and female, I could empathize with the oppressed but take no responsibility for their plight. It has just been only recently that I have realized how deeply that I too have been captivated by the sin of self-interest, saying "There but for the grace of God go I." This attitude is often found in the Christian Church (Disciples of Christ). How many of us would be willing to lay our lives on the line for the gospel of Christ?

This led me to conclude that Christian social concern requires not only that we ask what we should do in a broken world but also that we ask who we are to be. Therefore, I believe that the church of the 21st Century will be concerned with evangelism and conversion that is qualitative, effecting deeper and deeper changes in the hearts of persons, which will result in changes of sinful structures, economic systems, and political patterns in the global community. The issue will be not how many people we will have as members of the Christian Church (Disciples of Christ); rather, what kind of people we are as members of the church. Gordon D. Kaufman reflected on this need for a conversion of the human heart in his book, *Theology for a Nuclear Age*:

> Obviously, a dramatic and full transformation, a metanoia of our major social, political and economic institutions, of our ways of thinking and acting, is required. . . . It demands reflection on and action to bring about a metanoia in human life as a whole. . . . Devotion to God should help to break our loyalties to the less inclusive wholes and the more parochial centres of values to which we so often idolatrously give them in our ideological and patriotic and religious commitments.[9]

It is imperative that the church begin to be concerned with the conversion of nominal Christians to the gospel of Jesus Christ. A gospel that condemns the idea of self-idolatry for the sin that it is. Conversion implies the embarking of a new way of being in the world. I agree with Gustavo Gutierrez that conversion is not something done once and for all: "It entails a development, even a painful one, that is not without uncertainties, doubts, and temptation to turn back on the road that has been traveled."[10] What if the conversion of nominal Christians turned out to be the most effective means in evangelizing the non-churched?

This point is most vividly illustrated in the parable of the prodigal son, which is found in Luke 15:11-32. This is an old and familiar parable in which we have traditionally paid a lot of attention to the son who left home. However, the biggest challenge may not necessarily be reaching the one who left; rather, the son who stayed. It was this son who challenged his father's forgiveness and jubilation over the younger son's return home. The older son needed a conversion experience, a change of heart, in order to accept that God's love for us is not based on what we do, but rather who we are.

Ever since I became a member of this denomination, I have heard a lot of rhetoric related to the claim that we are a people of the Bible. It is time that we rediscover that tradition and that we begin to prepare and train not only our ministerial leaders but lay leaders as well, in new and creative means of teaching what the Lord requires of us. "What does the Lord require of you but to do justice, and to love kindness, and to walk humbly with your God" (Micah 6:8).

The issue of self-interest, which gives rise to an unequal distribution of resources, increased global militarization, racism, and sexism stands as the opposite of God's vision for humanity. The gospel proclaims the love of God for all humankind and the demand for justice for all. William Nottingham, in his book *The Practice and Preaching of Liberation*, put it this way: "In his own person, Jesus brings the forgiveness that enables us to start anew. The Holy Spirit works within us to implement love and justice."[11]

What can we, the Christian Church (Disciples of Christ), contribute to decreasing the suffering that will exist in our world in the 21st Century? We can begin by teaching a Christian faith that has the capacity to liberate and transform the hearts of people.

Notes

1. William M. Ramsey, *Four Modern Prophets*. John Knox Press, 1986, p. 63.

2. Robert Bellah, et al, *Habits of the Heart*. Harper & Row, Publishers, 1985, p. 285.

3. John MacQuarrie, *Principles of Christian Theology*. Charles Scribner's Sons, 1966, p. 239.

4. Jurgen Moltmann, *Theology of Hope*. Harper & Row, Publishers, 1967, p. 22.

5. Arthur Simon, *Bread for the World*. Paulist Fathers, Inc., and William B. Eerdmans Publishing Co., 1984, p. 34.

6. "Carter: Racism Could Be Inherent in All of Us." *Jet*, March 9, 1987, p. 15.

7. "Hate and Violence Mark 1986." *The Monitor*, March, 1987, pp. 1, 6.

8. Ruth Leger Sivard, *Women . . . A World Survey*, (World Priorities, 1985). Quoted by the Office on Global Education, Church World Service, "Facts: Women," October, 1985.

9. Gordon Kaufman, *Theology for a Nuclear Age*. The Westminster Press, 1985, pp. 45-46.

10. Gustavo Gutierrez, *We Drink from Our Own Wells*. Orbis Books, 1984, p. 95.

11. William Nottingham, *The Preaching and Practice of Liberation*. CBP Press, 1986, p. 38.

William J. Nottingham
President, Division of Overseas Ministries
Christian Church (Disciples of Christ)
Indianapolis, Indiana

A Truly Global Spirit

My purpose is to lift up just one of the essentials for Disciples renewal, as I see it. This has to do with the world mission of the church, which I am calling "A Truly Global Spirit." There will be three suggestions later on for areas of discussion.

I want to dedicate this paper to the memory of a French theologian, Georges Casalis, who died at the age of 70 on January 16 in Managua, Nicaragua, committed to the last in the service of the living word of God.

One of the books we'll hear cited frequently and wisely in these few days together is *Habits of the Heart* by Robert Bellah. It is remarkable that what gathers us together today as Disciples interested in renewal is equally his preoccupation as a social scientist! His concern is to say that religious faith has been the basis of community in America, to a great extent a positive factor in relating private and public life, and he shows that we are fast losing or have lost that basis of oommunity in a society of rampant and often tragic individualism. The expression "habits of the heart" (*les habitudes du coeur*) comes from the book written a hundred and fifty years ago by Alexis de Tocqueville translated as *Democracy in America*. "Habits of the heart" occurs in a context that goes on to speak of the different notions, diverse opinions, and the ensemble of ideas that also form the "habits of the mind" (*les habitudes de l'esprit*). Both are included in what de Tocqueville refers to as *mores*, and defines as: "The moral and intellectual state of a people." I think we have to deal with the *habits of the mind*, as we look at possibilities for Disciples renewal.

Bellah has rendered more of a service than we might realize, perhaps, because he makes us ask, "What was de Tocqueville really concerned about?" And the answer to that is political

67

developments in France. De Tocqueville knew that France as well as all of Europe in the 1830s was in for tough times, and he had high regard for what he thought was a good example in that part of Europe that had spilled over to North America. He believed in the power of religious faith to curb excesses of ambition and materialism in the life and death struggle underway in Europe between the masses of industrial workers and peasants, on one hand, and the enlightened, liberal, individualistic, commercial, and professional middle class, on the other. A good case could be made for saying that he was completely mistaken about the habits of the heart being able to control political interests with habits of the mind being what they were. But my point is that he looked at America to find how the *march of history* might possibly unfold in a way to mitigate the revolutionary demands of the poor and the repressive reaction of the rich.

For many different reasons, North America has succeeded in that better than some other places, so that here many of the poor of the past became the middle class. Democratic infrastructure was built into the system, not without struggle or disappointment, and thanks to religious freedom, habeas corpus, trial by jury, land for farmers, collective bargaining for workers, schools for the people (not just for the wealthy), emancipation, etc. But the developing storm that de Tocqueville saw for France and the rest of Europe in the early 19th Century goes on today in social struggles all over the world. The habits of the mind for Disciples must take that into account, and as we speak of *renewal*, the church cannot be unaware of or uninvolved in the sufferings and hopes of millions of people today. The habits of the mind must not misinterpret the continuing force of people's movements, human rights struggles, democratic demands to curb and redirect power, etc. The outcry of the oppressed is nothing other than the continuing historical process that produced both the Disciples and American democracy and apart from which we can only become marginal or reactionary.

One of our habits of mind is to think that something called "leftist" is a kind of anti-American label. What the terms "left and right" come from was the legislative assembly of 1791 in France, in which the party seated to the right of the tribune sought to preserve constitutional monarchy and those seated to the left of the tribune criticized the king and sought to lead the revolution to greater changes. Karl Marx was not even born until 27 years later! The division marked the interest not of the aristocracy that already had been defeated but of the middle class, people of property and power and a certain understanding of the republic on the *right*, and those who sided more with the people who had little or nothing to lose on the *left*.

And the political designations have swung between the two ever since. There have been many kinds of socialism apart from the Communists (including Robert Owen who debated with Alexander Campbell), even many different kinds of communist parties, the growth of religious socialism, social democrats, Christian democrats seeking reform, welfare states, and desperate forms of government planning, which developed along the way and appear around the world today. Disciples must understand what is going on in a long historical process that included two world wars, independence struggles against colonialism, revolution against feudalism, the growth of fascism, oligarchies and oppression, and the demands for farmland, housing, hygiene, education, employment, and prosperity that cover our globe.

A magazine has written: "The religious left is the only left we've got." What that means is not political ideology but that the religious community is one of the few places where there is real compassion for the poor and solidarity that will go as far as advocacy and sacrifice.

Our "habits of the mind" incline us to understand and sympathize with that movement towards relative liberation. I would rather emphasize that *positive* democratic and evangelical base among Disciples, which can be appealed to and which can grow in understanding and commitment concerning what is going on across our world—from the Philippines and South Korea to South Africa or Chile—and the way that half the world looks upon the struggle in Angola, Mozambique, or the People's Republic of China. The U.S.S.R. does not represent the solution any more than the United States does, but both do offer some forms of hope when their aggression is curbed. Both east and west are derived from the march of history to which Alexis de Tocqueville referred in the desperate hopes of the poor and the poor in spirit to transform their societies. Both the U.S.A. and the U.S.S.R. are repressive when the interests of the poor people are

69

perceived to be contrary to their own national interests, whether economic, military, or political.

We have all seen the reviews of the Broadway play *Les Miserables*, and we must remember that it was both Christian and revolutionary in 1862 when Victor Hugo wrote it. It must not be reduced to merely expensive entertainment in 1987. It must be allowed to call us to respect and sympathy for struggles for jobs and justice, food and freedom today.

Our "habits of the mind" must help us analyse sufficiently who we are as a people, the Disciples in the U.S.A. and Canada, and how we interact with rich and poor in our own society and across the world. Perhaps you heard this morning that one out of ten elderly in the U.S.A. are living in poverty! If we feel that there is a spiritual crisis in mainline protestantism, we must see also that it is part of a larger social crisis. It is related to culture, economics, modern secularism and the growth of militarism, with its fear and aggressiveness on one hand and guilty conscience on the other. It makes us ask the question of renewal, but not only of our denomination, as if we truly were a sect concerned only about itself and asking only internal questions, but about the society of which we are a part and in which we do represent something. This is the experienoe of the Division of Overseas Ministries, which is reporting for 1986 110 people in 31 countries, with more than 100 years' missionary history in Asia, 90 years' in Africa, 70 or 80 years in Latin America and the Caribbean. What I have described is a daily fact of life in churches we relate to around the world. With their reality of economic hardship and feudal domination our church has been in complete solidarity since the time of Archibald McLean and the Christian Woman's Board of Missions through the world mission of the church, which generates a "truly global spirit." Radical religious individualism, sectarian self-interest, neo-colonialism is somebody else's dream and practice, not ours.

At a deeper level, we are dealing with the relation between the self and the collectivity, which is working itself out in struggle and sacrifice in many different forms in every culture under the sun. I say "self and collectivity," using the words of Dr. Franklin Woo of the China Program of the National Council of Churches, because a philosophy of society adequate for the 21st Century must be aware of the insights and strengths of traditions very different from our own. Our tradition has come to include not only European but African, Asian, Hispanic American, and Pacific insights and strengths. Dr. Woo speaks of Confucian *guan xi*, with its own problems of patriarchalism and the preservation of the status quo, but which represents the relationship and obligation of the person to a larger wholeness. Rich and poor, people's movements, social justice, the pursuit of happiness are rooted in problems of relationship that our society has not solved and that are tied, in both conflict and cooperation, with other societies extended across the world. Professor Tu Wei-ming, former student of Robert Bellah and presently teaching at Harvard University, has written a book on *Confucian Thought, Selfhood as Creative Transformation*, which he considers to be an answer to *Habits of the Heart*.

Our task is to reflect good news in that process—the gospel of Jesus Christ—and to live in love, freedom, creativity, faith, and shalom (which means both justice and peace in all the prophets, including the prophet Jesus).

George Orwell wrote in 1946 that the world is suffering from some kind of mental disease that must be diagnosed before it can be cured. We diagnose the mental disease of our international life by saying that the sufferings of the poor are the motivation of a historical process that no one can hold back forever. And the gospel is our source of optimism about that, our commitment through faith in the resurrection to be on the side of *life* and not *death* and to have that faith in God, which brings joy to the task and beauty to the soul. I see the church as part of the diagnosis; but also out of its commitment and out of its understanding of suffering, especially in this time of Lent, the church can be an element of sanity, righteousness before God, and peacemaking that extends the horizons of every local congregation and gives new meaning to the communion in which we gather at the table of the Lord.

Where should Disciples look for renewal? I have three suggestions:

1. *A Rediscovery of the Bible.*

We need to remember where renewal comes from for Christians, where global awareness is portrayed, where a truly global spirit is given. Here is where the sending out of Jesus, the apostles, and the church is to be reflected on again and again. Here is where the eschatological vision of the reign of God is inclusive of the whole cosmos. When we speak of the world, we include the creation itself. That will figure more and more in biblical studies, as we express concern for the environment. And the Bible finds us in a different context from 1950 or 1930 or any earlier time. We know more about the Bible today, the scholarship is responsive to our situation, and the power of the word about sin and atonement keeps being renewed.

Not only in Latin America, but in Asia and in Africa and elsewhere, the suffering and struggling poor people have found a promise in the compassion of God. In Brazil there are 800 Base Ecclesial Communities involved in Bible study and in bringing change to their slum communities. They have met Jesus Christ in a new way, as one who favored the poor. Who can forget his description of heaven as Lazarus, the poor man, in Abraham's bosom? Not as compensation, but as God's preferential option for the poor, to use the expression of the Roman Catholic bishop's pastoral letter on economic justice. The eschatological promise of the Beatitudes turns the despair of the downtrodden to hope and joy. The Psalms ring with a new confidence for those who trust in the goodness of God. Disciples must find renewal in habits of the mind that enable the Bible to bring Jesus Christ to bear on our lives in a new way in this time. It must be central to our preaching. The lectionary ought to guide us. Our biblical culture must include a growing study beyond seminary and even a meditation and memorization that have passed out of usage. I make that point in the book for Christian Board of Publication *The Practice and Preaching of Liberation*, which I really wanted to call *Preaching As Mission*.

Let there be no mistake about it: The only renewal we can seek is that which comes from God, whose word and spirit are the means and power of life over death, of obedience over human sin, of peace and love over alienation and hate, of giving and sharing over oppression and indifference, of hope and celebration over despair and devastation.

What I like about Karl Barth is that he radically refused the cultural domestication of Jesus by the European middle class and fostered the philosophical recuperation of the God of faith, in other words revelation, spiritual joy, and grace as judgment and hope.

2. *The Use of Intelligence in Religion*

The second recommendation is to stand against the irrationalism of our times—that kind of petty thinking or refusal to think about basic issues, which is becoming so attractive in our society partly because it is easily marketable and appeals to the search for novelty and security. I don't just mean the "New Age" fascination that seems to settle in the Pacific Northwest, the channeling of figures from the ancient past, which has been on television recently, or the various kinds of separatist communities that exist. I mean the Disciples must find renewal in an expectation of intelligence in religion—ecumenical intelligence.

We must resist the tendency to have protestantism, let alone Disciples, defined by sectarians. That was the problem in the beginning! There are *ecumenical* conservative evangelicals, and the World Council of Churches is full of them, from the Lutheran Church of Norway to the Greek Orthodox or the Pentecostals of Chile. Our DOM works with Roman Catholics in Brazil and the Christian Apostolic Holiness Church in Zion in Swaziland, not because they are liberal but because they understand the oneness of the church of Jesus Christ.

There will be no renewal of the Disciples by lowering our ecumenical commitments. Intelligence has led us to the commitment to the wholeness of the church, so that we use the expression "not the only Christians," and we must see what a victory this has been. Even the powerful opposition is a tribute to its success. Institutionally there are some good signs; the union of Presbyterians and Lutheran bodies, as well as the Disciples and UCC conversations, have resulted from the ecumenical connection. I believe that a future generation will move beyond these present formations to new ecumenical vigor. Whether that is true or not, we must see that in action groups around the world, in prayer cells, in the prisons and hospitals of El Salvador, Christian unity is a *given*. It is taken for granted, as we work with Maryknoll priests and nuns or the Missouri Synod Lutheran Church in Central America.

Our roots are in the 18th Century, the Enlightenment, which not only produced Disciples and other streams of theological change in western European protestantism, but which produced the legacy of freedom of inquiry, human rights, scientific method, critical thinking, education, and forms of democracy that are

73

rooted therein. Leslie Newbigin has written about the dangers of
the Enlightenment, and of course we cannot compare the gospel
with the exaggerated expectations of progress through science
and technology, and all the rest that flowed from that period.
However, people still bring their brains to church, and I believe
that we have a particular responsibility to use the habits of the
mind that are native to us.

I think we have to realize in the context of American society
that the "secular humanists" are among our closest allies. Not in
their elementary conception of God and in their cynicism toward
the church, but in their acceptance of pluralism. For us, this lifts
up the importance of interreligious dialogue as a major agenda
item for the 21st Century in a world of growing interdependence
and coexistence in the light of God's grace.

The use of our intelligence cannot be surrendered in the next
generation. Even our spirituality should reflect the great intellectual mystics of the centuries, those who have enriched our culture,
our literature, our music, our science, and our way of life.

Intelligence brought us to the process of restructure in the
amazing unselfishness of the United Christian Missionary Society
to die for the sake of the larger church, even as the CWBM, the
Foreign and American Christian Missionary Societies before it.
That ecumenical intelligence must be honored among us.

3. *Solidarity with the Poor*

In the third place I call for renewal through an understanding
of the cry for liberation in the world in which we live. I have
referred above to the history that is going on around us and that
will prepare the world of the 21st Century for us to a large extent.
The question is not between right and left, so much as between
top and bottom, maybe between right and wronged, in most cases
a privileged minority and a desperately poor majority. When I
was preparing for this afternoon, I had before me the March 13th
New York Times financial section, where I read the following:
"As the stock market continues to climb, some eminent econo-
mists and financiers are dogged by the feeling that they are living
under a volcano, which could erupt at any moment—or lie dor-
mant for years. . . . We could easily enter a new, vicious circle
where dollar depreciation results in greater inflation, which in
turn necessitates a further depreciation. Everybody would wind

up a loser!" The article continues: "But a way needs to be found to escape from the straight jacket of an immobilized monetary and fiscal policy, lest the debt crisis of the third world, the over-capacity and unemployment of the industrial world, and the plight of commodity producers result in another depression." In the intervening two weeks, what if the world economic volcano had blown up? How trivial might become much that we had prepared to say! And I take that as further evidence that the Disciple community is related to the world beyond our doors and beyond our shores in a critical, crucial, inescapable way. There-fore, when the Latin America Council of Churches calls us to take stock of the external debt of their countries—$108 billion for Brazil, $53 billion for Argentina, etc., this is a concern for a church renewing the habits of the mind. Mexico pays $1 billion a month on interest alone. Poor Uganda: After years of Idi Amin, over half its export earnings are paid in interest annually! Both Brazil and Ecuador have declared in the last few weeks a morato-rium on their debt payments. The church leadership in these countries present that to us as their number one preoccupation. These heavy burdens increase the numbers of the poor, threaten the basis of democratic governments, make new productivity impossible, diminish the value of exports, and challenge the ade-quacy of our kind of social system for their kind of situation.

This same relatedness on a global level is certainly evident in the need for the church to educate and militate against nuclear arms escalation and other threats to world peace. Dr. Robert Gale, the physician who travels every month to the U.S.S.R. to monitor the situation of 469 survivors injured by the reactor explosion, said last June: "Chernobyl puts to rest any notion of an adequate medical response to a thermonuclear war." On a smaller scale, we have been led into one fiasco after another on the border of Nicaragua. We must see that as a great contradic-tion and tragedy. There can be no renewal for Disciples of Christ without repentance for the war with Nicaragua!

I am speaking about solidarity with the poor. We cannot enter into a conference such as this and not speak about stewardship. Disciples renewal has to take stock of the fact that offerings in 1986 amounted to $342,186,852 plus uncounted individual desig-nated gifts. Eighty-seven percent of that was used in the congrega-tion's own life and ministry! Among sixteen mainline Protestant bodies, we ranked fourth in per member average amount given ($423.76). Among these same sixteen, we ranked *last* in percent of mission beyond the congregation—including not just Basic Mission Finance but local mission and other causes as well—13 percent! About half of this was BMF for regional, national, and international ministries. In 1985, among 39 church bodies, we were 36th! That is worthy of attention when you realize that $277,000 came to Christian Theological Seminary through Basic Mission Finance offerings, and a million and a half dollars to our universities and colleges. It is important because it helps make things happen!

We have averaged 4.5 percent increases in giving in recent years, but DOM, along with many others, only received 1-percent and 1.43-percent increases. Our church life itself has become more expensive. We are using more and more of everything for ourselves! The *Together in Mission Program* to increase the level of BMF from $19 million to $25 million is underway right now. But we have to work at a higher proportion for others—as a renewal of our life together and ultimately our solidarity with the poor for the sake of Christ and God's reign, which is eternal.

We must be aware of the new program of the World Council of Churches called Justice, Peace, and the Integrity of Creation. Dr. Preman Niles, who was an ecumenical associate of our church in this city all last year, has been called to that office. Member churches, in whatever way is appropriate to them and whatever may be their relationships with the society in which they live, are to set justice, peace, and integrity of creation at the center of their world concern.

Tod and Ana Gobledale, missionaries to South Africa, told us a couple of weeks ago that "White South Africans expect us to think like them. They see only the color." It occurred to me that something similar is present here in the United States, where the public is not looking for the element of newness that the gospel brings in. It is always a surprise for many people when the "habits of the mind" are different because one's life is with God. But that is the difference that would really be renewal, not only within the Disciples community, but through it within our culture. We are just a minority of people, people who want to be part of a thinking person's church and people who, looking about them, have an understanding that the church is the mission of God sent into the world so that the world might participate in the divine life itself.

Conclusion: I see these three ingredients of a truly global spirit, which is one of the essentials of renewal:

1. A rediscovery of the Bible
2. The use of an ecumenical intelligence in religion
3. Solidarity with the poor

This is summed up for me in a statement that Dostoevsky, out of his Russian Orthodox spiritual heritage, wrote in a letter in 1854 (in the time of Alexis de Tocqueville and Alexander Campbell): "I would say to you myself that I am a child of this century, a child of unbelief and of doubt, up to the present time and even to the grave . . . . And yet, God sends me sometimes moments where everything is clear and sacred for me. It is in those moments, that I have composed a creed: To believe that there is nothing more beautiful, more profound, more lovable, more reasonable or more perfect than the Christ, and that not only is there is no such thing, but . . . there cannot be such a thing." I repeat: *nothing more beautiful, more profound, more lovable, more reasonable, or more perfect than the Christ.*

William O. Paulsell
President, Lexington Theological Seminary
Lexington, Kentucky

Where Disciples Should Look for Renewal:

Spirituality

I want to thank the faculty of Christian Theological Seminary for conceiving and developing the idea for this conference. This is a discussion that has been needed for a long time in our church, and I have high hopes that this will be an event of major significance for us. If we do not produce a Vatican II here, I hope future historians will look back on Indianapolis I as a turning point in our history and service to the whole church.

My assignment is to discuss the question: Where should the Disciples look for renewal in terms of spirituality. This is a topic very close to my heart, but it is a somewhat alien topic for Disciples. With a few notable exceptions, we have not developed a strong tradition of spirituality. We have developed strength in ecumenical leadership, in biblical scholarship, in preaching, and in church organization. In fact, I heard someone say recently that we have more polity than we do theology. We have had a historic commitment to social justice, to benevolence, and to foreign missions. We have produced outstanding leaders in these fields. However, while I find a good bit of interest in spirituality among Disciples these days, we have not yet developed the kind of leadership in this area that we have in other dimensions of our church's life. Yet, as I travel about and lead retreats for churches, ministers' groups and regional organizations, I find a hunger for a deeper spiritual life. By that I mean a hunger for some perception that God is present in human life, that God is present in the madness of a world that has already engineered its own destruction, that God is present in local churches, which frequently get diverted from their main purpose by issues that are painful and peripheral to the gospel. Where is this God about whom we hear so much from pulpit and classroom? Can this God be known, can a divine

78

presence be discerned at work within our lives? All other church questions pale into insignificance before this one.

I would like to approach this issue by using some of the terminology of Christian spirituality: *asceticism, mysticism,* and *ecumenicity.* Each of these terms refers to what to me are essential elements in any consideration of renewal.

I.

First, *asceticism.* The study of Christian asceticism is a fascinating activity. Throughout the history of the church we read of Christians seeking solitude in the desert, of Christians fasting and going without sleep and wearing hair shirts, of Christians practicing heroic forms of self-denial as they sought to purify themselves and clarify their perceptions of God. The roots of the word go back to the Greek *askesis,* which referred to exercise or training, such as an athlete might do to perfect skills. More popularly, the word is associated with the practice of self-denial as a form of penance or in an effort to move closer toward religious perfection.

We live in a different age, although there are still ascetics in the church today. Family life, the responsibilities of paying a mortgage, getting children through college, and preparing for retirement all mitigate against the simple austere life of the classic Christian contemplative.

Nevertheless, there is a lesson to be learned from this particular strain of Christian history. The lesson is that in order to have a clearer perception of God's presence we must free ourselves from many of the distractions that our culture would impose upon us and live by the values of the gospel.

The self-denial I would suggest as we think about the renewal of the Christian Church (Disciples of Christ) is that we deny ourselves the privilege of imposing American middle-class values of success on the church and stop treating it as a capitalistic enterprise. The purpose of the church, I would suggest, is to put people in touch with transcendence, to help people know the God who is at work in their lives with all of the implications that has for the way they live in the world. If you want to use more traditional language, it is our purpose to bring people into a saving relationship with Jesus Christ. To me that means living in communion with the divine so that we may do the will of God in a world of injustice, oppression, and self-destruction.

But we do not seem to judge the church in that way. We treat it as a capitalistic institution and impose middle-class values on it. We see it as a success if the plant is imposing, the budget grows each year, and the membership shows annual increases. We organize ourselves as businesses and measure success in business terms.

I have been interested in how Jim and Tammy Bakker have handled their recent problems. There was a day when a minister guilty of adultery was regarded as having committed a sin. But Bakker, borrowing a term from Wall Street, said that the whole problem was really the danger of a hostile takeover.

Pulpit committees want to look at the *Year Book* reports of ministerial candidates. Regional ministers complain of pastors who do not know how to read budgets, but God never seems to call anyone to a smaller church. I have two clergy couple friends who left what we might call a nice pastorate and opened up a small retreat center, which they run on a shoestring. When I asked them how the local clergy reacted to their new ministry, they said to me, "They just don't understand us because we are downwardly mobile."

I fervently hope that Christ will not say to me, "Sell what you have, give to the poor and come follow me." I find it impossible to live by, "Take no thought for tomorrow." I am made very uncomfortable by the admonition, "If anyone would come after me, let that person deny self, and come follow me." But these ideas are part of the gospel. Jesus does not bless the middle-class ideals of American life of upward mobility, prosperity, and endless consumption. We must not measure the church by those standards.

We need to take more seriously the radicalism of Jesus and try to understand it. If the church is successful by worldly standards, it may be because we have compromised the gospel and been unfaithful to its demands on us.

The reality is that the most important ministries carried out by our churches are often hidden and not measurable by statistical standards: comfort given during grief, hope offered in a hopeless situation, a word spoken or a deed done that gives a glimpse of God's presence, meaning given to a life that has known none. There is always the danger that the material success of our churches masks a lack of depth and the failure of a shallow theology.

Several years ago when a new Professor of Christian Education from a non-Disciples tradition joined the faculty of Lexington Theological Seminary, I brought her to Indianapolis to spend a day with the Christian Education staff at 222 South Downey. We had a very stimulating day and we were all enriched by it. At the end of the day our professor asked a question, "How do you know when you have succeeded in your work?" That is a basic question Disciples must ask. How do we know when we have succeeded? Is it when we have built more stately mansions, when budgets and programs have grown? The good that those things can produce is not to be denied, but let us not measure success in the church by the standards of the world. Let us develop a new vision of what the church can be, where success is measured by lives renewed, by values lived, by that regeneration that comes from the work of the Holy Spirit, by a clarifying vision of God. Let us measure success by an increase in justice, by the excitement of mission, by depth of commitment.

II.

This brings me to the second term from Christian spirituality that I would like for us to consider: *mysticism*. *Mysticism* seems to us an esoteric term, referring to experiences of visions, voices, and being lifted above reality into unspeakable mysteries. The term is defined in the *Oxford Dictionary of the Christian Church* as "an immediate knowledge of God attained in the present life through personal religious experience." *Religious experience* is a term that makes us Disciples pretty nervous. We are a rational people and take pride in that. The excesses of Cane Ridge repulse us, even if our roots are there. We are not comfortable talking about religious experience. We do not tell people when we were saved or how we were converted.

In evangelism we often try to sell people on the church program rather than talking about new life in Christ. We are more at ease promoting youth groups, fellowship dinners, and air conditioned sanctuaries than we are in encouraging a search for transcendence. I would like to suggest that one element in our renewal must be a concern for the ways in which people experience and know the presence of God.

There is certainly no one way in which this happens. God may be known in solitude, or God may be known in the interaction between people in a community. But, to use very outdated language, we need to engage in a serious study of the soul, that is, how humans can know the divine, how creatures can know the Creator. It is one thing to believe in God. It is another to know a divine presence experientially. What did the early Christians mean when they said, "We have seen the Lord"?

I want to applaud several members of the faculty of Christian Theological Seminary at another point, and that is in bringing out a new book of worship for the Disciples, *Thankful Praise*. The renewal of worship must be a high priority for us. I see our leadership in public worship as an effort to make it possible for people to experience transcendence. A good worship service provides a context for this.

But beyond that, I would urge a recovery of the sense of the mystery of God. My complaint about fundamentalism is that the answers are too easy; they are all there. All one must do is find the right verse of scripture to quote. I am impressed, however, in studying the classical Christian mystics, how the closer these people come to a knowledge of God, the less specific are their statements about God. Those who have the deepest spiritual lives are overwhelmed with mystery.

Our worship services must not be simply the presentation of a set of propositions; they must communicate and elicit from us a sense of awe, a sense of that overpowering mystery, which we label God, but about which we know so little. There has been much emphasis in recent years on worship as celebration. That is a great emphasis, but I would urge us also to lift up the sense of awe that comes from being overwhelmed with mystery.

So that is the second source of renewal I would suggest, the tradition of Christian mysticism. We need to study how people have known God over the centuries, how valid the contemplative claims are, and what the impact of that has been on human life. If God cannot be known, we are not preaching the truth. But if humans can experience the divine in the midst of life, we need to learn how that can happen. To live by the guidance of the Holy Spirit it is not required that we be tongue-speaking charismatics. We need to study how to evaluate religious experience and discern its validity. This kind of work must be at the heart of our church. After all, our ultimate goal must be new life in Christ.

III.

This brings me to my third point, which is *ecumenicity*. We are nothing if not ecumenical. We have always had a deep yearning for the unity of the church. This is the part of our heritage of which I personally am most proud. At the level of spirituality, we need to search the whole range of the Christian tradition for help. Roman Catholic monasticism, Lutheran pietism, Quaker silence, Methodist holiness, and Orthodox mysticism all have much to teach us.

This is already happening. At two aftersessions at the Des Moines Assembly, several of us discovered that there is a significant number of Disciples who have studied the classics, who have spiritual directors, and who are drawing on the riches of whole Christian spiritual tradition in their personal lives. There is a treasure house of religious experience just waiting to be explored. We must overcome whatever prejudices we might have about other Christian traditions, for anyone who has known spiritual reality and had a contemplative knowledge of God is someone from whom we can learn.

Our study must be critical. We cannot accept without question any claim to religious experience. But there is so much that happened between the Book of Acts and the "Declaration and Address" that is worthy of study in our churches. This study of the varieties of Christian experience could be a major source of renewal for us.

But there is another dimension. Many of us are becoming aware of the global dimensions of our faith. There has been significant Christian renewal in the third world. While that experience is not ours, there should be something we can learn from those who see God at work in situations that appear on the surface to be hopeless. If, in the midst of oppression and suffering, people sense the presence of God, that experience is something we must examine and from which we can learn.

But there is another level to the global dimension of religious faith. We must break out of the limits of the Christian tradition and look at the total religious experience of humankind. While to the Western World the Christian tradition has had the greatest appeal, there are other parts of the world where far different, and sometimes much older, religious traditions appeal to millions of people. How does a Hindu, a Buddhist, a Moslem, a Jew, or a Native American experience transcendence? What do they mean when they talk about religious experience? We cannot ignore the fact that people practicing religions other than ours also experience a divine presence and develop their lives accordingly. The discernment of God's presence would seem to be a common human experience. There are mystics in virtually every known religion of any importance. Again, we must not be uncritical, but we must acknowledge that the experience of transcendence is not limited to Christians. Confrontation with mystery is common to all humankind.

I would suggest that we drop the debate about which religion is right and which is invalid and look instead at human experience. How do men and women experience transcendence, how do they know the divine, no matter what symbols or stories they use to conceptualize it. There is a common human experience of God. As Urban T. Holmes said in his *History of Christian Spirituality*, "To say that human beings are spiritual creatures is to suggest that they are capable of possessing the presence of the life-giving God."[1]

It was expressed in an interesting way in one of my favorite books on philosophy, Robert Pirsig's *Zen and the Art of Motorcycle Maintenance*:

> The allegory of a physical mountain for the spiritual one that stands between each soul and its goal is an easy and natural one to make. Like those in the valley behind us, most people stand in sight of the spiritual mountains all their lives and never enter them, being content to listen to others who have been there and thus avoid the hardships. Some travel into the mountains accompanied by experienced guides who know the best and least dangerous routes by which they arrive at their destination. Still others, inexperienced and untrusting, attempt to make their own routes. Few of these are successful, but occasinally some, by sheer will and luck and grace, do make it. Once there they become more aware than any of the others that there's no single or fixed number of routes. There are as many routes as there are individual souls.[2]

If Disciples seeking renewal would be truly global, let us study the experience not just of Christians, but of all religious people to see if there is some insight, some glimpse of spiritual reality that we might gain.

So, these are my suggestions for where we should seek renewal in the area of spirituality. First, let us practice self-denial and see the church in other than middle-class, capitalistic terms. Let us deny ourselves the right to evaluate what we do in terms of plant, budget, and growth, but let us emphasize those intangibles, those unmeasurable items that make the difference in human life. Let us evaluate the church in terms of lives changed, faith deepened, justice achieved, God known. A church that says no to the world's standards of success may be more faithful to the gospel and a more powerful Christian witness. The last sentence in Reinhold Niebuhr's wonderful journal of his pastorate in Detroit is, "If the church can do nothing else, it can bear witness to the truth until such a day as bitter experience will force a recalcitrant civilization to a humility which it does not now possess."[3]

Second, let us emphasize the knowledge of God, intimacy with the Divine, as the foundation for what we do as a church. Let us draw on the whole range of Christian experience as we seek to learn how people have known and experienced the reality of God over twenty centuries of Christian history.

Third, let us be truly global in our outlook and learn what we can from the basic religious experience of humankind. The time for religious exclusivism in our outlook is over. Now is the time to be truly ecumenical, truly worldwide, truly global in our religious quest.

I believe that among Disciples there is a hunger for more depth in church life. Budgets and organizations and programs do not satisfy religious longings if their purposes are purely humanistic or secular. If we are going to preach that God is real, we must help people find that reality in their own experience. Such an effort would call on our best theological resources. If we could have any success at all, I believe we would experience a significant renewal.

Notes

1. Urban T. Holmes, *A History of Christian Spirituality*. Seabury Press, 1981, p. 1.

2. Robert M. Pirsig, *Zen and the Art of Motorcycle Maintenance*. William Morrow, 1974, pp. 187-188.

3. Reinhold Niebuhr, *Leaves from the Notebook of a Tamed Cynic*. Harper & Row, 1980, p. 198.

Clark M. Williamson
Professor of Theology, Christian Theological Seminary
Indianapolis, Indiana

Theological Reflection and Disciples Renewal

I. Introduction

A cursory examination of the literature of the early period of the Disciples movement discloses that Disciples identity initially clustered around a set of theological convictions. Central to our movement were claims about the authority of Scripture (usually expressed as the "ancient gospel" or the "ancient order of things"), the right and duty of private interpretation, the commitment to Christian unity, and a set of social-moral goals: the improvement of educational systems, the elimination of injustices from the political system, and the abolition of slavery. Also prominent was the doctrine of justification by grace through faith, to which Campbell referred in *The Christian System* as "the test of a standing or falling church" (Campbell: 153).

For whatever complex of reasons having to do with our history, we Disciples have by and large lost most of these early convictions. Mainline Disciples felt, after the struggle with Disciples scholasticism, that Campbell's restoration principle was legalistic and abandoned it. We dropped the Scripture principle rather than reinterpret it, and thereby lost a critical ability to examine our church life and teaching in the light of a norm of appropriateness. We remembered the right of private interpretation more than the duty of it, and interpretation degenerated into mere opinion. Now we delight in a diversity of opinions, forgetting that to interpret is to understand, and that to understand is to be able to give reasons. Diverse understandings can be discussed in a community of faith. Opinions can merely be asserted. Consequently, moral stances as well as theological ones tend to be looked upon as opinions and as such make no claim on those who regard them. We have no widely accepted norms of appropriateness or intellectual and moral intelligibility. It is not surprising that in place of God's justifying grace, works-righteousness often rears its ugly head in our popular literature.

We have retained at least a verbal commitment to Christian unity, but we do not tie it together with reinterpreted norms of appropriateness, intelligibility, and moral plausibility, i.e., we have lost the theological conviction that it is only as a witness to Christian unity that our own life is justifiable. Hence, by and large, that witness itself tends to become verbal while *de facto* we have become comfortable with being a denomination and are immediately concerned more with the struggle over diminishing slices in the declining denominational pie than with the witness to Christian unity.

II. A Case for Thinking Theologically

Surely, then, if we are to recover from the malaise that seems to have settled upon our life together, we need to recover the willingness to think theologically about how to make the Christian witness. Doing so might contribute to our ability to sustain a critical and imaginative approach to church life, indeed to proclaiming the gospel. Given our proclivity to dismiss theological proposals with the comment that we would not want to make them "tests of fellowship," the course of wisdom dictates that first we make a case for thinking theologically before turning to the question of how to do so.

The reason we ought to think theologically is that we are human beings. The anthropologist Clifford Geertz views religion as "a semiotic concept of culture," by which he means that a religion is a symbol system of form of culture by means of which people communicate, perpetuate, and develop their knowledge about and attitudes toward life. Geertz regards the human being "as a symbolizing, conceptualizing, meaning-seeking animal" whose "drive to make sense of experience, to give it form and order, is evidently as real and as pressing as the more familiar biological needs." In short, religion provides orientation for people who cannot live in a world they cannot understand.

Religion, therefore, is a specific kind of synthesis or "fusion," having two aspects to which Geertz refers as "ethos" and "world view." It is never merely metaphysics because "the holy bears within it everywhere a sense of intrinsic obligation: It not only encourages devotion, it demands it; it not only induces intellectual assent, it enforces emotional commitment." Nor is religion ever merely ethics, because "the source of its moral vitality is conceived to lie in the fidelity with which it expresses the fundamental nature of reality. The powerfully coercive 'ought' is felt to grow out of a comprehensive factual 'is,' and in such a way religion grounds the most specific requirements of human action in the most general contexts of human existence" (Geertz: 140f., 126).

The ethical, normative side of religion reflects "the underlying attitude toward themselves and their world" comprised in the life of a people, and the metaphysical side embodies elements expressed in "their picture of the way things in sheer actuality are, their concept of nature, of self, of society." Because the two aspects are fused, the way of life is justified, made "intellectually reasonable by being shown to represent a way of life implied by the actual state of affairs which the world view describes, and the world view is made emotionally acceptable by being presented as an image of an actual state of affairs of which such a way of life is an authentic expression" (Geertz: 126f.)

Although both aspects are essential to human beings and to religion, Geertz asserts a certain priority of world view to ethics. The need is for a metaphysical grounding of ethics, for the "ought" to grow out of an "is." Yet religion is a fusion of world view and ethos, never merely one or the other, and not merely both, but what Schleiermacher called "the necessary and indispensable third." Religion functions to provide a metaphysical foundation for morals and to express the moral meaning of the metaphysical.

Hence religion asks and answers the question about the meaning of ultimate reality for us, a question simultaneously about both ultimate reality and ourselves. Religion compromises the deepest spirituality—the existential question of how we understand and constitute ourselves in relation to ultimate reality—and the deepest morality—the question and answer as to how we are empowered to work for the liberation of the neighbor. Therefore the concerns represented in this plenary session are grievously misapprehended if they are taken to be alternatives to one another.

We who stand in a particular religious tradition think theologically because we always have to grapple anew with the issue of who God is and who we are given and called to be and because we must do this in a manner appropriate to our tradition and intellectually and morally plausible. This task is given us with our humanity because how we are human is a matter of how we determine to understand ourselves and to live.

III. How We Think Theologically

As we turn to the question of how we think theologically, an autobiographical point may be helpful. I grew up in a Disciples congregation of which my grandfather was the pastor. After I had been teaching theology for a few years, I had the good luck of reading his papers and learning how fundamentally I was shaped in the Christian life by that congregation and by his teaching. It is a bit humbling for a professor of theology to find all his deepest commitments expressed in the notes for sermons he had heard (when he was listening) as a boy. The Christian tradition was passed on formatively to me in that congregation, but not in a way that was without problems. When I was in high school I had that delicious crisis of faith that we all ought to have (preferably before coming to seminary). That crisis was composed of two questions: What the church proclaimed sometimes did not make sense in the light of the rest of what I knew (the world view issue) and the church did not seem to mean what it said morally on questions of race (the ethics issue). Little did I know it, but I was beginning to think theologically, which we do when we cannot correlate with one another the tradition that is handed down to us and the situation in which we find ourselves.

The task of everyone who is a minister and therefore a teacher of the Christian faith (which you will remember Alexander Campbell said is the task of the minister) is to interpret the situation in which we live in the light of the tradition and to reinterpret the tradition in the light of the situation. The tradition has to be reinterpreted if it is to answer the question posed by the situation, and the situation has to be reinterpreted to make visible the significant question(s) that it puts to the tradition. What keeps the tradition a vital source of faith and life is that it is critically appropriated in each new historical situation.

We take responsibility for our Christian tradition or for our little corner of it, therefore, when we do theology in the church, that is, when we *criticize* the way in which we make our Christian witness. Because many people regard criticism as destructive, let me add that to criticize is simply to think, to subject to rational review. We criticize not to destroy but in order to test because we want what we test to stand. We need to see that the Christian faith can stand up to questioning, because it itself claims to tell us the truth about God, about the world, about the neighbor, and about ourselves.

The distinction between making the Christian witness and thinking about it is not a separation: Those who make the witness cannot fail to think about what they do, and those whose main task is to think about it do so because they are concerned to make that very witness in a way that is appropriate and credible. Also, it is a relative, not an absolute, distinction, a matter of emphasis. In those moments when we do theology, our primary function is to criticize the way the witness is made. But this is done in the service of making the witness, which task we take up in the myriad ways in which we teach the Christian faith.

To think theologically is to criticize the witness of the church in the light of two questions: (1) whether we are being appropriate to our tradition and (2) whether we are being intelligible. The first critical question is whether this or that piece of Christian witness is *appropriate*, that is, whether it is indeed *Christian*. The standard of appropriateness is the gospel of Jesus Christ: the gracious promise of the love of God offered freely to each and all and, therefore, the command of God that justice be done to each and all of those whom God loves. The gospel is not a circle with one center but an ellipse with two foci: God's radically free grace and God's command of justice. When Christian witness forgets God's absolutely free grace, it falls into works-righteousness; when it overlooks God's command that justice be done, it comes to grief in cheap grace. When it overlooks that God's grace is offered to *all*, it becomes exclusivistic and refuses to let God be God.

The stress on God's radically free grace recognizes the truth of the Reformation principles *sola gratia, sola fide*, by grace alone, by faith alone. Our justification is *by* God's grace, appropriated *through* our response of faith. The emphasis on the transcendence and all-inclusiveness of God over and beyond all finite realities, including the church, observes another old theological principle: *ad majorem dei gloriam*, all our witnessing and thinking is to be done to the greater glory of God.

The second criterion in the light of which the theologian reviews the witness of the church is intelligibility. Intelligibility is a two-pronged idea, entailing (1) theoretical as well as (2) practical-moral intelligibility. We will deal with them in this order.

The (1) witness of the church must be comprehensible—we must be able to understand it if it is to speak to us (although our understanding needs to be transformed by the Christian witness, the result is nonetheless a transformed understanding) and it must be true. So we ask what a statement "means." And once we are satisfied that it is meaningful, we then ask whether it is so and how it is so. Christian witness must be intelligible in these senses: It must be comprehensible, free of contradiction, coherent, and possessed of illuminating power. What Paul calls "the truth of the gospel" (Galatians 2:5) is not something to which confusion and falsehood can bear witness. The gospel is God's liberating truth: ". . . you will know the truth and the truth will make you free" (John 8:32). Christian witness to God's liberating truth must itself be true, worthy of being believed. It does not suffice to say that this witness must be meaningful, for the simple reason that many meaningful statements are false—we could not know they were unless they were first meaningful. Hence the Christian witness must be not only meaningful but true; we must be able in the words of 1 Peter "to give a defense (*apologian*) to everyone who asks of you a reason (*logon*) concerning the hope that is in you" (3:15).

The question (2) whether a way of making the Christian witness is morally plausible is answered by applying to it the norms of moral thinking: equality, freedom, the dignity of the human person, the adequacy of a proposal to the situation it addresses. Sexism, racism, and anti-Judaism in the church indicate the need for the Christian witness to be not only appropriate and intellectually plausible, but to be morally plausible as well. A church that self-contradictorally proclaims the love of God for each and all with its words and hymns, while turning a deaf ear in matters of practice to women, blacks, and other minorities is simply not making a morally believable testimony.

The function of theology—to review the witness of the church in the light of standards of appropriateness to the gospel and of intellectual and moral plausibility—follows from the nature of religion as that was characterized earlier in this paper. Alfred North Whitehead commented:

> Rational religion is religion whose beliefs and rituals have been reorganized with the aim of making it the central element in a coherent ordering of life—an ordering which shall be coherent both in respect to the elucidation of thought, and in respect to the direction of conduct towards a unified purpose commanding ethical approval (Whitehead: 30).

Whitehead's study of religion led him to see that a particular faith arises from some moment of disclosure, from which it draws its ideas. Yet it asserts that these ideas are "of universal validity, to be applied by faith to the ordering of all experience" (Whitehead: 31). "The great instantaneous conviction in this way becomes the gospel, the good news. It insists on its universality, because it is either that or a passing fancy" (Whitehead: 133). Furthermore, religion cannot admit that its central notions are "merely pleasing ideas for the purpose of stimulating its emotions . . . ; religion is the longing for justification. When religion ceases to seek for penetration, for clarity, it is sinking back into lower forms" (Whitehead: 83).

The theological payoff of these insights comes in H. Richard Niebuhr's *The Meaning of Revelation*. Quoting Whitehead on rational religion, Niebuhr defines revelation as "that part of our inner history which illuminates the rest of it and which is itself intelligible" (Niebuhr: 93). Says Niebuhr:

> The special occasion to which we appeal in the Christian church is called Jesus Christ, in whom we see the righteousness of God, his power and wisdom. But from that special occasion we also derive the concepts which make possible the elucidation of all the events in our history. Revelation means this intelligible event which makes all other events intelligible. . . . Revelation means the point at which we can begin to think and act as members of an intelligible and intelligent world of persons (Niebuhr: 93, 94)

Christian theology is the effort to understand and interpret the Christian faith in a way that is (1) appropriate to the gospel of Jesus Christ and that is (2) intelligible in the dual sense of enabling us both to think (intellectually) and to act (morally) as the ecclesial community.

IV. Campbell and Disciples Today

Bearing in mind these considerations, we turn to Alexander Campbell, asking to what extent he was aware of such matters. If to think theologically is to criticize how the church makes the Christian witness and to propose alternatives derived from the same norms in the light of which one has exercised criticism, Campbell was clearly a theologian. The standards in the light of which he did his thinking were: (a) a formal norm of appropriateness that was his version of the Reformation *sola scriptura* principle; (b) the doctrine of justification by grace through faith, which was his and the Reformers' material norm *sola gratia, sola fide*; (c) a concern for intelligibility, which he usually framed in terms of the interpretation of Scripture; and (d) a concern for the moral life of Christians and of the Christian community, understood as arising from the command of the gospel. Let us look briefly at his treatment of each of them.

Campbell (a) had a high doctrine of scriptural authority, yet he unswervingly affirmed that the language of scripture is "*human* language . . . to be examined by the same rules that are applicable to the language of any other book, and to be understood according to the true and proper meaning of the words, in their current acceptation, at the times and in the places in which they were originally written and translated" (Humbert: 42). He rejected as an "ultraism" the contention that the Scriptures claim a plenary and verbal inspiration for themselves. "It would be a great reproach upon the Evangelists to represent them as believing every jot and tittle of the words of the Messiah and of themselves to have been inspired, when not any two of them narrate the same parable, conversation, sermon or aphorism in the same words" (Humbert: 43). He characterized the Bible as "but a specific embodiment of the Holy Spirit. It is veiled spirit or limned grace; and hence, the Spirit works only through the word upon the understanding, the conscience, and the heart" (Humbert: 43). Because it works upon the heart, it requires to be appropriated by the whole person; because it works upon the understanding, it requires to be understood; because it works upon the conscience, it requires the leading of a new life of repentance. The word that is the norm of appropriateness itself requires to be appropriated intellectually and morally.

Campbell's rules of interpretation should be more well known among Disciples than they are. They call for considering (1) the historical circumstances of the peculiar book of the Bible being read, (2) the author and the people addressed, (3) use of the same philological principles applied to other literature, (4) the use of common usage or context to decide the meaning of words, (5) understanding the nature of trope, (6) ascertaining the point of parables, symbols, etc. His last rule is: "For the salutary and sanctifying intelligence of the Oracles of God, . . . *we must come within the understanding distance*" (Campbell: 3-4). An uninterpreted, unintelligible scripture cannot function authoritatively.

Yet the function of scripture as canon is to limit the options that are open to the church in matters of belief and practice; the early church adopted a canon of scripture precisely to rule out alternatives. Campbell, too, used scripture in the sense of canon, saying that "whatever is of the faith, of the worship, of the morality of Christianity, was both possible and necessary to be promulgated; and is expressly and fully propounded in the sacred Scriptures. The law of expediency, then, has no place in determining the articles of faith, acts of worship, nor principles of morality. All these require a 'thus saith the Lord' in express statements, and the sacred scriptures have clearly defined and decided them" (Campbell: 72-73). To the requirement of an express precept of the Lord, Campbell also added what he called "the apostolic tradition" (Campbell, 1901: 64) or "the universal practice of the early church" (Campbell: *passim*).

In Disciples history the role of scripture as canon was defined, in our scholastic period, in an increasingly legalistic way. Since Disciples have (largely) rejected legalism, the role of scriptural authority among us has been ambiguous. We need to recover a credible form of the function of scripture as canon—as a norm of appropriateness—for our time. Campbell's insistence on the centrality of hermeneutics to the understanding of scripture can greatly assist us in this enterprise. Yet in a church that rightly celebrates its diversity, we cannot lay down one hermeneutical approach or one definition of the canon as the only legitimate option. The most that we can say is that if Disciples are to be a community of faith, we must all be ready to give reasons for the scriptural norm of appropriateness that we propose. Without a lively discussion of what is and is not appropriate in the church, we find ourselves in a situation in which anything goes and in which we begin to wonder about our identity.

Campbell's (b) material norm of appropriateness was the doctrine of justification by grace, through faith, a norm that stood in some tension with his formal scripture principle (a tension that also marked the work of the Reformers of the 16th Century). Adequate appreciation of the fundamental importance of the gospel of God's justifying grace could have saved Disciples from the twin perils of legalism and moralism, as it could still. Campbell rightly understood that the gospel is dipolar, involving the promise of God's love graciously offered to each and all as well as God's command that justice be done to each and all of those whom God loves. He knew that we are justified by God's grace, not by our faith, not, as he said, *"on account of faith, as though there was in faith some intrinsic merit"* (Humbert: 137). Making "faith alone" a ground of justification, said Campbell, is as Pelagian as making works or beliefs such a ground. Yet God's justifying grace frees us to do the works of justice on behalf of the neighbor, and thereby makes us responsible for doing them. Campbell worked out the relation between them in this way:

> Sinners are justified by faith, and Christians by works. But this is too laconic for the mass of mankind. It is one thing, however, to introduce a person into a state of acceptance, and another to live acceptably in that state. It is one thing to enter into the married state, and another to make a good wife. Now faith in God's promise through Jesus Christ, is argued by the apostles, as that which brings men into a state of intimacy, friendship, . . . acceptance with God. Thus faith is accounted to a man for righteousness, by the mere favor of God. But the continued enjoyment of such a state is by the same favor made to depend on our behaviour. (Humbert: 142)

If we understand what we mean when we say that we are saved by grace, we will see that all of God's overtures to us are gifts: "The messiah is a *gift*, sacrifice is a gift, justification is a gift, the Holy Spirit is a gift, eternal life is a gift, and even the means of our personal sanctification is a gift from God" (Campbell: 20). All these bespeak God's free favor toward us, and all that is required of us is "to accept them freely, without any price or idea of merit on our part" (Campbell: 21). There are conditions of enjoying such gifts, such as cordially accepting them, but no conditions of merit.

In spite of this strong emphasis in Campbell, Disciples history is loaded with moralism and legalism. The authentic Disciples spirit is genuinely ecumenical toward all other kinds of people, but legalism and moralism always turns nasty, and among Disciples they wipe away everything for which we stand. The reason for this is simple: Legalism and moralism turn God's gracious gift into a condition apart from which God is not free to be gracious and apart from which we are not prepared to be gracious. Both define those who do not meet the condition as outside the sphere of God's grace and our moral concern. If Disciples today are to recover their identity as a people witnessing to the all-inclusive love of God graciously given, and to recover our vitality as a people energized to do justice by that same grace, we desperately need to salvage our awareness of the gospel of God's graciously given love as the only ground of our justification and transformation. Then we can be freed from the embarrassing legalisms and moralisms that vitiate our witness to Christian unity.

Therefore, to think theologically today as Disciples will require that we critically reappropriate and reinterpret the formal and material norms of what is suitable for Christians. Similarly, we shall have to renew our concern for (c) the intelligibility of our witness. As we cannot live in a world that we cannot understand, so we cannot live by a faith of which we cannot make sense. Very simply, to understand is to know what to do next. Not to understand is not to know what to do next. If the justified are to live by their faith, they must know what to do next. As Campbell put it, testimony must be "made credible before it can be relied on"; "a testimony *confirmed*, and yet *incredible* to those to whom it is tendered, is a contradiction in terms" (Campbell: 97, 99).

Campbell claimed that reason was to exercise the same jurisdiction over testimony that it exercises over objects of sense perception (Humbert: 18), and that there can be no "real conflict between faith and reason" (Humbert: 19). "Reason is that eye of the soul to which the light of revelation is addressed" (Humbert: 22). While Campbell argued that salvation is not in the act of believing but in the object or proposition believed, he nonetheless contended that "the power of faith is the power of truth" (Humbert: 24). But "no truth can have power over either the heart or the hope" of people "that is not understood" (Humbert: 25).

This truth that we are to understand is that "we are saved by *grace*" through faith. Faith "is no more that the belief of [this] truth; and it is evidence alone that ascertains and demonstrates what is truth" (Humbert: 28). This truth is of a strange sort, however, being the truth about a person—the person of God in Christ; belief in it, therefore, "is a person believing, trusting, loving, obeying, and rejoicing in a person—viz. Jesus Christ" (Humbert: 26). One cannot believe *in* a person without believing *that* some statements about that person are true. Yet merely to believe that certain propositions are true of a person without knowing the person is to commit the fallacy of misplaced concreteness. We Disciples have so downplayed theology that we sometimes construe faith in the person of Christ as having all the theological content of a hiccup. Perhaps a quotation from Campbell will help:

> While . . . faith is the simple belief of testimony, or of the truth, and never can be more nor less than that; as a *principle of action* it has respect to a person or thing interesting to us; and is confidence or trust in that person or thing. Now the belief of what Christ says of himself, terminates in trust or confidence in him: and as the Christian religion is a personal thing, both as respects *subject* and *object*, that faith in Christ which is essential to salvation is not the belief of any doctrine, testimony, or truth, abstractly, but belief *in* Christ; trust or confidence in him as a person, not a thing. We take Paul's definition of the term and of the thing as perfectly simple, intelligible, and sufficient. For the term faith, he substitutes *the belief of the truth*. (Campbell: 37)

Further, Campbell's developed view of the meaning of truth in *The Christian System* opens up for us a way to deal with truth in a pluralistic context. He claims that to confirm a testimony, to verify it, is "to make it credible to those to whom it is tendered," to give to those who hear it "power to believe" (Campbell: 98). He further notes that this must be done differently for different people.

Campbell seems to recognize that the notion of truth has a context invariant force—it is what we have power to believe or what is worthy of belief—and a context dependent meaning—how people in one time and place understand it will differ from how people in a different time and place understand it. This is a way of confirming our concern for truthfulness without falling into either an absolutism that insists that there is only one way of making sense of the Christian faith or into relativism that delights in the conflict of diverse "opinions" while taking none seriously as making a truth claim. We prize liberty and diversity of judgment highly, not because we are not concerned for truth but because we recognize that nobody has a corner on the market of truth. Many voices need to participate in our theological conversation, the voices of those hitherto silent or oppressed as well as the voices of all of us.

But the other side of this coin is also important: If we claim that what we say is worthy of being believed, then it is incumbent upon each and all of us "to make it credible to those to whom it is tendered," to give our sisters and brothers inside and outside of the church the power to believe it. We have to reject all lazy pluralism and repressive tolerance, which manifests a deep lack of concern for Christian truth, and replace them with a strenuous conversation in which anybody's views are just as worthy of being believed as they can be shown to be believable. If we begin to take seriously our responsibility to be credible, perhaps we will become a community that can talk about its faith, a community of faith. We cannot long fail to take seriously the great Christian beliefs.

We have said that our Disciples witness must be interpreted in the light of critical norms of appropriateness and intelligibility, and that intelligibility entails not only an intellectual but also a moral component, that our witness must be (d) morally plausible. Our church today is wracked by a contradiction at this point. On the one hand, Disciples are well aware of most of the contemporary liberation theologies. Feminists keep before us the concerns of feminist liberation theology, and black Disciples rightly do not let us forget the claim on justice that they make. Through the work of the Division of Overseas Ministries and Disciples in the poorer nations of the world, we are kept aware of the voice of third-world liberation theologies. We are less attentive to the theological movements concerned with the liberation of the ecology from destructive exploitation and concerned to liberate Christian tradition from its inherited anti-Judaism, although some Disciples are also committed to justice in these respects. Nevertheless, overall Disciples do a better job at attending to the moral dimension of the Christian witness than of attending to its appropriateness and intelligibility. On the other hand, and here is the contradiction, our church is still beset by an individualistic understanding of salvation and of the church that fails even to comprehend the voices that bespeak the need for a morally plausible praxis of the Christian faith in our time.

As religion enables us to understand the world in which we live and to know how to act in the world so understood, so the gospel tells us of God's love graciously offered to each and all and of God's command that justice be done to each and all. Therefore our witness in each generation must be morally intelligible; Campbell argued that to come within the understanding distance means having a "moral soundness of vision" (Campbell: 5). We study the deeds of God to which the Scriptures bear testimony "intent only to know the will of God" (Campbell: 5). From the things done by God graciously on our behalf we learn "the reasons of all piety and righteousness, or what is commonly called religion and morality" (Campbell: 6). While true faith is the belief of truth, "the *power* of faith is also the . . . moral meaning of the testimony, or of the facts [gracious acts of God] which the testimony presents" (Campbell: 93). God's grace empowers us, frees us, motivates us to do justice to all those whom God loves: "*God never commanded a being to do any thing, but the power and motive were derived from something that God had done for him*" (Campbell: 150).

In Campbell's theology there is what we might call a double movement of liberation, comprised on the one side of redemption and on the other of emancipation. Sinners are redeemed from their alienation from God by grace and thereby empowered to work for the emancipation of the neighbor from injustice. Says Campbell:

> Indeed, the strongest arguments that the Apostles use with the Christians to urge them forward in the cultivation and display of all moral and religious excellencies of character are drawn from the meaning and value of the *state* in which they are placed. Because forgiven, they should forgive; because justified, they should live righteously; because sanctified, they should live holy and unblamably; because reconciled to God, they should cultivate peace with all . . . , and act benevolently towards all;

because adopted, they should walk in the dignity and purity of sons of God; because saved, they should abound in thanksgivings, praises, and rejoicings, living soberly, righteously, and godly, looking forward to the blessed hope. (Humbert: 146)

Campbell reminds individualists that God's grace makes moral behavior necessary and liberationists that God's grace makes moral behavior possible. In the Reformation tradition, false religion consists always in throwing us back on our own resources, of telling those who are curved in upon themselves that they must love the neighbor and the stranger and do justice toward them, or of telling them to imitate a pattern disclosed in the words and works of Jesus. Christ comes spiritually to the Christian every day; he brought life and liberty to light then, and he brings them now. The advent of Christ is the time of grace and the gospel, of the Word and of faith. Faith in God's grace redeems us from ourselves and makes us available to our neighbors. Campbell can help us remember, therefore, to ground our moral practice, in whatever forms we propose it, in the only way appropriate to Christians, in the all-inclusive grace of God. Thereby we might be delivered from the twin perils of self-seeking individualism and self-flagellating moralism. Meanwhile we must be as open to varied ways of making moral sense as we are to varied ways of making theoretical sense, and as ready to back up our varied proposals with good reasons in this area as in the other.

V. Conclusion

The church essentially is and ought to be a transfigured way for human beings to live in community. Made up of a plurality of people and cultural traditions, it is grounded on the apostolic tradition and its witness to the God of a unique promise and a unique command made known to us in Jesus Christ. In the church, privatistic, narrow, and authoritarian ways of living together are in principle overcome, and in it is actualized, at least fragmentarily, a universally gracious love that frees us from sin, estrangement, and oppression. The church is an anticipatory sacrament of the coming reign of God, as well as a vehicle of God's contemporary grace.

When the church quits thinking theologically, when it ceases to discipline its life by critical self-reflection, it tends to lose its ecclesial existence and to proceed aimlessly toward becoming a privatistic, alienated association of people providing such services as the relief of psychic distress and institutional maintenance. One source of our renewal assuredly lies in recapturing the ability to think theologically about our common life.

Bibliography

Campbell, Alexander, *The Christian System*. Standard Publishing Company, 1901.
Geertz, Clifford, *The Interpretation of Cultures: Selected Essays*. Basic Books, 1973.
Humbert, Royal, ed., *A Compend of Alexander Campbell's Theology*. Bethany Press, 1961.
Niebuhr, Richard, *The Meaning of Revelation*. Macmillan, 1941.
Whitehead, Alfred North, *Religion in the Making*. Macmillan, 1926.

Nadia M. Lahutsky
Assistant Professor, Texas Christian University
Fort Worth, Texas

Can an Ecumenical Church Be Evangelistic?

It Had Better Be!

I have been asked to address my words this morning to a question that goes like this: Can an ecumenical church be evangelistic? It's a curious question, one might even say a preposterous question. But I am not going to say that, not just yet. What I am going to do is ask you to join me in a little journey, a journey I hope will be an exercise in self-discovery (a reappropriation of our tradition if you will) and one that will force us to think about ways of being *church* appropriate to the 21st Century.

We must first ask the questions: Who are we? What are we? These are fundamentally important questions. They are the kind of questions each of us must ask of ourselves (and answer successfully) if we are to manage many of the life decisions that come our way. They are questions we must ask if we are to present ourselves authentically to the world around us.

I was a graduate student in the late 1970s, at a time before demographic patterns shifted and when the predictions of experts were that only 10 percent of us (that is one out of every ten) in graduate programs in the humanities would be hired to teach. That was a depressing statistic, and even all of us—students in the humanities though we were—could tell what the numbers would mean for us. Consequently, each of us went off to job interviews with a heightened sense of the importance of the upcoming event. Each job interview was "a nibble," and you couldn't afford to blow it, for you might not see another one of them. The clown among this group of erstwhile college and seminary teachers sent us off to our various interviews with what I think is memorable advice. I offer it to you in a slightly sanitized version. Russell said, "Be yourself, unless you're a jerk, in which case you should be someone else." At first the one who heard this sage advice would roar or giggle at the absurdity of it. Then, the sober face would appear, as the listener realized that, to a certain extent, the successful outcome of the job interview depended not just on answering each question appropriately. Getting the job might have something to do with who you were. It's about your identity. That is to say, it's not just what you do and its effectiveness; it's also a question of what you are and its worthwhileness, if you will, of your value.

If you will not find this piece of advice too silly, I hope to demonstrate its value for our discussion here today. But for it to contribute to our discussion, we must modify it somewhat. Let us take a restated version of it. "Be yourself, unless you're a jerk, in which case you should be somebody else." "Be yourself, that is, be the kind of church you have been in your best modes, unless that makes you unfaithful to the gospel in our day, in which case you, we, this church deserves only to sink into oblivion."

Well, I do not think the historic expression of the Christian faith that is now called The Christian Church (Disciples of Christ) is a betrayal of the message of the gospel. That is not to suggest that it is a perfect expression of the gospel. But it is to say that it has made a witness worth preserving in and for our world.

So, then, let's explore the question of our identity—who we are and whether it warrants a future—before we look to see if this creature can be evangelistic. What are those characteristics without which we would not be us, but somebody else? I submit that they are three. Probably another list could be made, but I imagine these would appear in some form. Who and what are we? (1) We are a biblical people; (2) we are a reasonable people; and (3) we are a people who evidence a powerful impulse toward Christian unity. Let's look at these in turn.

Of course, we are a people of the book. It is important to us that our beliefs and practices be consistent with the Bible, especially the witness in the New Testament to God's special revelation in Christ, but not, I hope, to the exclusion of seeing God's work in the history of those with whom God first made covenant. To say we are a biblical people does not for us today mean that we expect to find in the verses of the New Testament a precise blueprint for our churches today. To do so would likely mean being either blind or very disappointed. If we have found difficulties in the old Restorationist hopes for reproducing primitive Christianity, that need not signal an abandonment of the Bible. What it does mean is that we are free to reexamine our assumptions about the Bible and thus bring ourselves into direct dialogue with the Bible itself. That is, I would argue, more life-giving than dialoguing only with a *tradition about the Bible*. It cannot mean that we take the Bible less seriously; indeed, it dare not, for we have chosen not to pass on to our children any particular concrete traditions about the Bible. We had better be giving them the Bible itself, with its testimony to God's continuing faithfulness, and in all its wonderful variety and disturbing vagaries. We had better be letting them know that *this is their story too*. No doubt more could be said. I will assume that more has been said on this point in various corners of this meeting already and that more will be said before we all leave. In any case, surely all can agree with my claim that, as Disciples, we are a biblical people. I ask: Do you want to give this up? Do you want to be somebody else? I hope not.

I have claimed that a second characteristic of our identity as a church, is that we are a reasonable people. I know, from the tone of discussion in the interest groups here and at some General Assemblies, that you might dispute this! Nevertheless, The Christian Church (Disciples of Christ) movement and the institution have been characterized by a willingness to put the affirmations of faith of our mothers and fathers to the test of reason. In other words, we have not easily accepted the authority of tradition, in the form of creeds or ecclesiastical structure, if it did not seem to meet the needs of the gospel message in our day.

Again, none of us wants to hear anyone say that it doesn't matter what you believe, that one person's ideas are just as good as another's. We have, no doubt, heard the "I'm entitled to my opinion" defense. These are insipid and wrong conclusions drawn from a profound theological claim. To be a reasonable people is for us to recognize that there is always a kind of tenuousness to one's collections of words. It is to remember that no matter how saintly the one who gave expression to a point of faith, the words are just that—words. They lack the finality of God's truth, and thus cannot be held as binding for all time if they should of themselves no longer persuade hearers.

We heard yesterday about this—the faith must be credible—in the plea made by Clark Williamson. Another way of saying this is that membership in The Christian Church has not required the checking of your brain at the front door or before the baptistry. Another William said this also. We have held it acceptable for individuals and groups to engage in the task of reconsidering the traditional affirmations of faith in light of contemporary developments in the sciences and changes in social attitudes. In fact, I understand a substantial part of our past to include a willingness to engage in frequent intellectual exchanges, and not just as exercises in abstract thinking. The lively theological debates among our forebears were for the purpose of identifying the nature of authentic Christian identity in their day. The level of discussion we can find among the Campbells, Stone, Errett, and Garrison, among others, puts us to shame. The pablum we offer today through our publications presupposes an anti-intellectualism foreign to our heritage. It presupposes an unwillingness on the part of our people to think. I consider that presupposition to be rubbish. And I base my view on the willingness I have encountered among our people to sink their intellectual teeth into very difficult ideas and issues, without flinching or squirming. If anything is in need of our best thinking, it must be that faith that we hold dear!

Do we not find in our tradition a willingness to put reason to work for the benefit of the faith? Why else did Disciples plant so many colleges and institutes around this country? Is this association of the love of learning and the desire for God no longer of value to us? I ask: Is it a part of our identity that we would give up in order to be somebody else? I hope not.

Third on my list of characteristics essential to our identity is our historic commitment to the cause of Christian unity. In the minds of many 19th Century leaders, it was tied directly to restorationist hopes. If we can only get back beyond all these divisive historic creeds and unbiblical church offices and requirements, we will surely find a church on which all Christians can agree. Such a wonderful hope and such a hopeless dream! You and I know today that we can no more return in naivete to the first century— no, no more than the United States and the Soviet Union can simply put behind them the last seventy years of mutual acrimony. The past cannot be erased, no matter how much the current affliction of historical amnesia among our young people seems to work to the contrary. We may not know our own history, but it exercises its effect on us nonetheless. We can never go back to the kinds of relations that Wilsonian America had with

Czarist Russia. (Who would want to?) But let us all pray that it is possible to go beyond this current era of "Evil Empire" vs. capitalist devil.

In a like manner, we cannot go back to the 1st Century and pretend that if we just look hard enough, we will find neutral and mutually acceptable definitions of terms like *presbyter, bishop*, and *deacon*. It's too complicated for that. We may not all be able to narrate the journey by which today's Christian groups reached their peculiar definitions, but we would be fools to ignore those definitions and to ignore the realities of history.

What, then, does it mean that we are a people characterized by a desire for Christian unity? First off, since I seem to be specializing in negative meanings today, allow me to say what it isn't. It does not mean anything like the lazy ecumenism of: "Well, it doesn't really matter which church you belong to, since they're all equally valid." Clearly, some churches are more equal than others. It does not mean: "The decline of religion in the modern world requires Christians to cling to each other like battered and dislocated persons, orphans in a hostile world." Well, I do not believe the children of God have been abandoned by their Creator and Sustainer. If we feel like orphans, maybe it's because we haven't been listening to the right prophets.

So, what then does this historic commitment to the unity of the church mean? First of all, we see it in the aching awareness that we experience, even when we all get together, that we are not complete. We know, perhaps subconsciously, that as long as the body of Christ is broken, we cannot imagine ourselves to be whole.

Second, it contains an awareness that our way of being church is itself imperfect, at best incomplete. Just like those words and phrases used to express the faith, our understanding of church must have a provisional character to it. We must be willing to allow our vision and experience of being church to come under questioning, to be critiqued by others whom we proclaim also to be in Christ. I am convinced that we must remain open to what we can learn about being church from our contemporaries who are in Christ and from those who have preceded us—and by those I mean all, ever, baptized into Christ. By means of this second characteristic, we are protected from the danger of seeing only ourselves and thinking that we constitute the whole.

106

Finally, it means that we as a body must continue to offer the kind of steady and responsible leadership we have long given to the modern ecumenical movement. In a very real sense, it is *who and what* we are; it alone would be, I think, a significant justification for our continued existence as a body. The reason I say this has to do with what I earlier called a reality of history. In our day, the efforts to mend the cracks in the body of Christ are most effectively happening in formal ecumenical circles.

Does it mean we canonize everything that the World Council of Churches does? I think not; for this body, too, comes under our critical principle. Does it mean that we commit ourselves to *Baptism, Eucharist, Ministry* without qualification? Probably not, for we will ask that this product of the modern ecumenical movement be tested by the whole people of God. Do we commit ourselves to the process by which it is tested? I hope so, for it is the ecumenical reality of history given to us. To pretend otherwise is to misread the signs of our times. Now, I know that meetings and documents and journals can be boring and appear to be lifeless. But remember that the life of the ecumenical movement is to be found in the struggle of theological exchange in which men and women bound together by the Holy Spirit seek to discover ways to make visible their relationships. What you find in any document or journal is already a couple of steps away from the source of life. If you would see its lifeblood, translate the exchange to the local congregation, where you can watch those who are in Christ struggle with what it means to say we are in Christ and to take seriously the claims of others. It can happen, I tell you, for I have been a part of such discussions and felt the Spirit's presence.

To know that in and of ourselves we are not whole, to recognize that our ways may not be God's ways, to tell the world through our actions, through our life together, that God's plan for creation is wholeness and not brokenness—this is, I think, what it means to say that Disciples are a people committed to the cause of Christian unity. I ask you: Do you want to give that up? Do you want to be somebody else? I hope not.

What, then, do we do with this identity of ours? How do we live it out in our world? More specifically, to address the issue assigned to me for today, can we be a biblical, reasonable people, committed to Christian unity, and an evangelistic people when the common wisdom today tells us these pieces don't belong together any more, that ecumenical churches are not evangelistic, that this is an either/or option?

At this point, we must again ask the question of identity. "Who are we?" This time, I wish to answer the question from a different angle. Who are we? Or, Whose are we? We are Christ's; we are a people rescued from our sin and alienation and brought into bonds of reconciliation with God and with each other. This, obviously, is an answer that gets closer to our innermost nature. We are Christ's, and because we are Christ's we are transformed—no longer left to our own resources alone (it's nothing you have to do); no longer stuck in our patterns of guilt and self-recrimination; no longer orphans. We are not orphans, because we have been adopted into God's family, made brothers and sisters one with another and with all others adopted by God's love. This family, unlike most human natural families, demonstrates limitless fertility. The resources necessary to support this family come from an unlimited supply—God's boundless love. Having been ourselves the recipients of such astonishing and unwarranted love, having been ourselves drawn from isolation into community, from sin to forgiveness, it is inconceivable that we would then seek, even unwittingly, to limit that community.

But the further question remains: Do we believe this? Do we actually live our lives in such a fashion as to give witness to God's astonishing love for us? If we do, then we must be a church that is evangelistic! For the message of the gospel, that God has already loved you and given you family-member status, is not one that allows itself to be boxed for domestic consumption only. To refuse to take the message to others is to refuse to believe the message, for it does not want to be confined to any one group— congregation, denomination, color, ethnic identity, social class connection, country, or whatever.

I'm not sure how long I can get away with saying the same thing in different ways. But I think I'll keep at it a bit longer. Once more: If we believe that God's love has already overcome the alienation of human existence, (or at least given us a foretaste of such), then our lives are touched with a transcendent meaning. We are not necessarily more important than those who have not heard this message and do not, therefore, know of their adoption, but we possess a different perspective on the vicissitudes of life.

We can see our lives in the context of a larger plan, God's plan for all the creation. We can find in the message of the gospel a salve that brings wholeness to our lives. We have identified a transcendent purpose for our lives and a presence that serves to heal our hurts. As we heard yesterday from Paulsell, this is a telling of people that God is real—the first step before helping people find that reality.

We share this sense of purpose and offer of healing with the world around us (if we believe it), not because it brings us any rewards—but because we cannot do otherwise. If we lose this center to our being, if we lose the willingness to proclaim the gospel in our day, then nothing much else will matter—not sophisticated counseling methods, not extensive social service activities or community organization efforts, not warm-hearted Sunday school classes, not detailed evangelism programs, not more elegant music and more formal worship, not more contemporary music and more informal worship, not gymnasiums and family life centers to attract youth, not singles groups and young marrieds groups and young marrieds with children groups (did I leave anything out? Probably). None of this will have anything other than temporary results if it does not come out of what we truly believe about what God has done for us and for all.

I have resisted trying to make a list of how-tos here, for I believe that task properly belongs to the deliberations of the working group. What I have tried to do is make clear that we really have no choice. For, you see, I do believe that the question is a preposterous one. The question is not, "Can an ecumenical church be evangelistic?" For us the question must be, "What do we have to do that we have perhaps not been doing to make clear to the world that an ecumenical church must be evangelistic?" In fact, would you not want now to revise my earlier given list? Are we not, by definition, as a people—biblical, reasonable, committed to Christian unity, and evangelistic? I ask you. Do you want to give these up in order to be somebody else? I hope not.

T. Garrott Benjamin, Jr.
Senior Minister, Light of the World Christian Church
Indianapolis, Indiana

Can an Ecumenical Church Be Evangelistic?

Can an Evangelistic Church Be Ecumenical?

I want to thank God for the vision and vitality of the members of this seminary community in bringing us together around so noble a purpose as "reappraising the Disciples tradition for the 21st Century." We have come to gain insight, inspiration, and information on our identity as Disciples as well as to pool our ideas for future focus as faithful followers of Jesus Christ.

My task is to address the questions: "Can an ecumenical church be evangelistic? Can an evangelistic church be ecumenical?" At the outset, let me answer with an emphatic "Yes!" to both questions. The Church of Jesus Christ, to which we all belong as Disciples, must be "ecumenically evangelistic *and* evangelistically ecumenical." This is both the challenge of the Great Commission and the original purpose of the Disciples movement, which according to Garrison and Degroot was not simply to be a "great people (however great they may become), but to propagate simple evangelical Christianity and to bring to realization the principle that the "church of Christ upon the earth is essentially, intentionally, and constitutionally one."[1] As Disciples, we would agree to this affirmation intellectually, but *practically* we continue to find that we have great difficulty living it out. And our difficulty is often exacerbated by our failure to reach common ground concerning the definition of terms. We need to first look at the definitions of the terms *church, ecumenical*, and *evangelistic*. We need to look at our present dilemma and we need, also, to determine direction for the future *because our present form* of church life has become a major hindrance to the work of evangelism.

Let us first look at what me mean by church—that beloved community (visible and invisible) where Jesus is Lord and every man and woman is a brother and sister. The World Council of Churches' landmark document *A Theological Reflection on the Work of Evangelism* defines the church (in terms of the Nicean Creedal statement) as being "one, holy, catholic, and apostolic," terms that are not simply "institutional but instead descriptions of the distinctive Christian life that should shine through the institutional shapes."[2] The W.C.C. document is even more definitive as it gives the four marks of the church in relationship to the servant-ministry of evangelism. These include the idea of the church as one, holy, catholic, and apostolic.[3]

In light of this description, the ecumenical movement has no other intention but to promote Christian unity as expressed in John 17:21: ". . . that they all may be one." There are some who would define the ecumenical church as a "faith free-for-all" and a movement of "ecu-maniacs" whose sole purpose is to reduce the church to a theological "melting pot" where identity is lost and inspiration is gone. Even though I believe that in all movements there are those who abuse that movement's purpose, I also believe that we should not "throw the baby out with the bath water." If we mean by the term *ecumenical*, "The Church of Jesus Christ living beyond the barriers of broken humanity as a sign of God's purpose of reconciliation," then I think we all can shout "Hallelujah," and if not "Hallelujah," then in the same spirit of unity, we can say "Amen!" I am not talking about polite piety leading nowhere but a righteous radicalism that W. A. Visser't Hooft, leading 20th Century ecumenist, has called a "spiritual battle for truth" and not a battle of brothers and sisters based on the assumption that one is right and the other is wrong. It is a *common* battle against *error* and ecclesiastical arrogance. It is a dialogue between *equals*.[4] It is the foundation of Christian unity and the key to effective evangelism, for how can a divided church speak comfort and healing to a broken world?

In Dean Kelley's important study, *Why Conservative Churches Are Growing*, he basically concluded that an ecumemical church will not grow because "social strength and leniency do not seem to go together."[5] I do not want to underemphasize the relevance of this book, but with this thesis I disagree. I do not believe that being ecumenical erodes evangelistic efficacy. I believe that ecumenicity and inclusiveness enhances evangelism by sharing the life of the church with those who do not look, act, or think like us.

111

It makes the church even more attractive because it brings in with it creative tension that can give the church style and substance as well as liberate the church from a preoccupation with maintaining the status quo.

To be ecumenical is by nature to be evangelical because it calls for "unity *with* diversity" and "unity *without* uniformity." It demands that our *witness go beyond those who act like us, look like us, and think like us*. Paul states in Romans 14 that we ought be be able to "disagree without being disagreeable" because "none of us lives to himself, and none of us dies to himself. If we live, we live to the Lord, and if we die, we die to the Lord; so then, whether we live or whether we die, we are the Lord's. For to this end Christ died and lived again, that he might be Lord both of the dead and of the living" (Romans 14:7-9). And to this end, we commit ourselves. However, even as we do this we need to broaden our perspective on ecumenism. James H. Cone is instructive here.

> When the World Council of Churches was formed in Amster-
> dam in 1948, the term ecumenical had acquired a modern mean-
> ing that referred to "the relations between and unity of two or
> more churches (or of Christians of various confessions)." This
> definition remained dominant in theological and church con-
> texts until the recent appearance of highly articulate and radical
> theological voices of Asia, Latin America, and Africa and its
> diaspora. Third World theologians began to insist on a defini-
> tion of ecumenism that moved beyond the traditional intercon-
> fessional issues to the problems of poverty and the struggle for
> social and economic justice in a global context. In their attempt
> to connect ecumenism with the economic and political struggle
> for a fuller human life for all, Third World theologians also
> began to uncover the original amd more comprehensive mean-
> ing of the term (*oikoumene*) ecumenical. In the Greco-Roman
> world generally and also in the New Testament, (*oikoumene*)
> referred to the whole inhabited world and not simply religious
> activities. With this broader perspective in mind, it is appro-
> priate to apply the term ecumenical to "both secular and reli-
> gious aspirations toward achieving a united human family living
> in harmony with its global habitat."[6]

Theologian Jurgen Moltmann argues that the church should work through the ecumenical movement to expand its range of "human unlikeness," thereby demonstrating the love of God in Christ for all humanity and enhancing its ability to make disciples of *all* nations and peoples. We need to move from the idea of "melting pot" to the reality of a "sanctified salad." A "sanctified salad" represents Christians who bring their individuality and differences together to enhance unity and not to erode it. A salad becomes a salad only when the individual ingredients stand on their own in the same bowl. The modern church seems to want its "onions" and "cucumbers" to be the same. This is self-defeating. Our churches are full of "look alikes" that worship alike, whine alike, and decline alike. Instead, we need to inspire inclusiveness and delight in diversity, realizing that it contributes to the vitality and vigor of the church as well as giving distinction to our tradition as a people who sincerely believe and practice "unity without uniformity." The sooner we do this the closer we will be to reflecting the will of God for the church in our time—a "world house" church that demomstrates unconditional love without regard to (but regard for the interpretations and perspectives of) race, color, creed, or national origin, where Jew and Gentile, African and Afrikaner, master and servant, male and female, white, red, yellow, and brown, have and have not, educated and uneducated, degree and no degree, Ph.D. and "no D," can sit together at the Master's table. Anything less than this kind of inclusiveness winds up leaving the church parochial, provincial, and powerless.

The ecumenical church is not evangelistic when it insists on exclusivity and uniformity. If necessary, *it must disrupt fragile "like-minded" unities* in order to achieve the unity of Christ in its fulness. Let me illustrate by what has happened in terms of black Disciples and white Disciples. Out of the pain predicament of a separate and structurally racist movement known as the Disciples of Christ, whites and blacks entered, some twenty years ago, into a fragile structural unity that is not working in the best interest of the *whole* church. It is unfair and unthinkable for a church with a 96 percent white constituency to talk about meaningful integration with so small a black constituency. No matter how well intended and no matter how many quotas are filled on national boards and regional committees, the problem still screams at us. The problem is that size-wise, "whales" and "minnows" have little in common except that they both swim. If the church is really serious about evangelism, it could never allow that condition to exist. The "minnow" is so busy surviving in the presence of the "whale" that it never gets a chance to work on its own agenda without its diversity being challenged as "non-whale." Let the "minnow" grow and develop to its full stature, *then* let's truly come together as one. Simply stated, to be "pro-minnow" is not to be "anti-whale" and to be pro-black is not to be anti-white. We need not be intimidated but inspired by the authenticity and ultimate strength this freedom will bring to our movement. Martin Luther King Jr. has said: "I can never be what I ought to be until you are what you ought to be and you can never be what you ought to be until I am what I ought to be. This is the interrelated structure of reality."[7]

The evangelistic church must be ecumenical because the object of the Great Commission demands no one be excluded from the claim of Christ and the proclamation of the gospel. The evangelistic church must be ecumenical because it is living proof that Christ lives and reigns. It establishes Christian credibility because John 17:21 states even further, ". . . that they all may be one . . . that the world may believe that thou hast sent me." It really is not so much "converting the converted" as it is conversing and coalescing to discover that which is essential that we can agree on, and what is nonessential that we disagree on, and being able, in the process, to demonstrate that we are all Christians by our love. This will send the non-evangelized world a message of hope, instead of the "mess" of bickering denominations competing for members in the name of Christ.

We have tried in our local church to take seriously the "evangelistically ecumenical" challenge not only in the class and color complexity and diversity of our congregation, but even more so in our call to discipleship. We do not call for members to join our church alone, but our call is for people to "come to Jesus"—into the body of Christ primarily, and the local church of their choice secondarily. Our membership is taught this as our evangelism thrust, and our Sunday morning invitation to Christian discipleship expresses this exactly. Let me illustrate by the story of the trapeze artist who never missed the connection with the swinging bar. He said, "My secret is to 'shoot beyond the bar' and as a result, I never miss." We need to "shoot beyond the bar" in our evangelistic efforts—beyond membership and beyond church growth. Instead of trying so hard to get folk to join our churches, we need first to introduce them to the Liberator. We need committed Disciples in the fold, and not just church members added to the roll.

Our churches are too survival-oriented. We are operating out of the fear of decline instead of the bold and daring faith of disciples of Christ with faith in a great and Sovereign God who has done great things. National church leaders seem to demand all-out loyalty to the structure and the system rather than to the Scriptures and the Spirit. We are often viewed as a church of committees rather than a church of the committed. As a result, our churches, in spite of our rich heritage of diversity, turn out to be "look alikes"—overwhelmingly "white," basically rural, and determinedly "dry." Intellectually, we know what the church ought to be and we symbolically demonstrate it, but this conference will always be under the shadow of conclusions reached primarily by "look alikes."

As we look with confidence toward the 21st Century, we need to look back and get perspective and then go forward in faith. We need to go back (not in time but in commitment) to the theological and biblical certainty, the lordship of Christ, and the preeminence of the Scriptures that made us strong. There is no substitute for basic Bible study, biblical and expository preaching, and prayer and fasting. They go hand in hand *with* a commitment to the social justice issues. Cone and other black theologians rightly note that "black church people contend that the search for unity in Jesus Christ cannot be separated from the struggle for justice in society."[8]

This holistic approach will give new life to worship and witness. What happened to "Where the Scriptures speak, we speak, and where the Scripture is silent, we are silent. Bible names for Bible things and Bible things in Bible ways"? (We see little meaning in having the Bible as a "textbook" even in this conference.) This *is* our identity but it has simply become a slogan without significance because we have fallen into a rut of rationalism, which supports "sameness" and denies diversity. We need aggressive local leadership and committed national leadership in these areas. If we ever began to recover and reclaim the Bible as "the Book," Jesus as Lord, and the pastor as the leader, the training of the laity, and soul-winning as the way, our churches would take on new life.

Our worship should reflect our evangelistic ecumenism and our inexpressible enthusiasm. We need to touch more and feel more. We need to clasp our hands in joy and open our mouths unto the Lord in worship in loud "Amens" and shouts of praise. This is not as much pentecostal as it is a perspective on biblical praise that is visible, vocal, and audible. Every now and then I think my white Disciples brothers and sisters are incapable of the emotional dimension of holistic worship, but then I see them before a forty-inch screen and an I.U.-Syracuse game and "shazam"—transformation! They praise their team with loud and gutteral sounds; they stand on their feet, clap their hands, and shout for almost two hours. Can we not transfer a portion of that enthusiasm into our worship of the King of Kings? Why, you ask? Because it opens the door of inclusiveness and welcomes in the "others," and because we desperately need a springtime in our church, whose "winter of discontent" has become a way of life. It is time for a change lest our legacy become known as the "chosen frozen."

It's time for a change that calls for a balance between not only a personal salvation and social action but also the best in ecumenism—which we have described not as cheap pluralism or paternalism, but a church taking seriously the interpretative "world-house inclusiveness"—and the best in evangelistic Christianity, which promotes an orthodox view of the historical Jesus as Lord of life, to whom "every knee shall bow and every tongue confess" that he is Lord, and who compels followers to go into all the world and preach the good news of Christ. We ought to be able to link our hands in protest of apartheid in South Africa as well as lift our hands in praise of the Savior. We must know who we are in Christ as recipients of God's grace and not possessors or purveyors of it. We must remember that the ground is level at the foot of the cross and that judgment must be reserved for the one who sits in the judgment seat.

The unity we seek is from above. It is the unity authored by the Holy Spirit. There is no conflict between ecumenism and evangelism in the Spirit. Let us pray that the Holy Spirit will be allowed to breathe on our church and this conference with the hope that our lives and ministry will be renewed in deed as well as word. This cannot happen unless each one of us, male and female, black and white, yellow and brown, conservative and liberal, charismatic and rationalist, evangelical or liberal, submit our individualistic persuasion to the one who knows no labels and who says, "You shall receive power when the Holy Spirit has come upon you; and you shall be my witnesses in Jerusalem and in all Judea and Samaria and to the end of the earth" (Acts 1:8).

Let me conclude by saying that my comments are not meant to be absolute, because we have all brought something to this conference. For the last twenty years I have shared this basic message with our church. I may not be right, but I have been consistent. I love the Christian church universally, The Christian Church (Disciples of Christ) particularly, and the Light of the World Christian Church most especially. I love the church so much that I am willing to share this constructive critique with you. You do not have to agree with it, but as a good Disciple you're bound to respect it. I still have faith in the future and in you. Otherwise, I would not be here. The growing disenchantment must be stopped. I believe this week has signalled a new beginning.

Brothers and sisters, we need power from above. We have the significant sayings. We have the social conscience. We have the trained clergy. We have the sanctuaries and seminaries. We have a great heritage, but we need power to open our hearts, our minds, our mouths . . . to clap our hands, fall on our knees, and to repent of reverse fundamentalism and self-righteousness, while we take hold of our neighbor and sing together liberation's theme song, "We shall overcome. Deep in my heart, I do believe. We shall overcome someday." It is with this hope that I believe we all can face the future with confidence.

Notes

1. See Winfred E. Garrison and Alfred T. DeGroot, *The Disciples of Christ: A History*. Christian Board of Publication, 1948, pp. 11 and 150.

2. Colin Williams, *Where in the World*. National Council of Churches, 1963, pp. 56-57.

3. *Ibid.*, p. 56.

4. See Michael Kinnamon, "Truth and Community: Restoring the Ecumenical Vision." *Encounter*, 48:1 (Winter, 1981), p. 129.

5. See the Discussion of Kelley's theory in Dean Hoge, "A Test of Theories of Denominational Growth and Decline," in Dean Hoge and David Roozen, eds., *Understanding Church Growth and Decline: 1950-1978*. Pilgrim Press, 1979, Chapter 8.

6. James H. Cone, *Speaking the Truth*. Eerdmans, 1986, p. 142.

7. Cited in Lotte Hopkins, *"I Have a Dream": The Quotations of Martin Luther King, Jr.* Grosset & Dunlap, 1968, p. 79.

8. Cone, *Ibid.*, p. 143.

117

Joan B. Campbell
Executive Director, U. S. Office
World Council of Churches
New York, New York

The Passion for God's Future

Isaiah 65:17-25
Acts 1:6-8
John 13:34-35

"A new commandment I give to you, that you love one another; even as I have loved you, that you also love one another. By this all [people] will know you are my disciples if you have love for one another."

This is a time to give thanks and to credit those who have influenced our ministries. I want to bring a unique word of thanks, and it will tell you something about what has informed this particular sermon. I want to thank the World Council of Churches for my education. I want to thank all of those people from around the world who have let me come into their homes and into their lives. I want to express my gratitude to all who shared their suffering and their pain and their joy with me and educated me in the way which I now know. Come with me on a mind journey of this world. Let us visit God's children—that family that we are commanded to love, even as we have been loved.

Our ticket doesn't take us everywhere, but let us stop first in a refugee camp in Lebanon. People are huddled together, talking in hushed tones, waiting, waiting and wondering when the next disaster will strike. They ask one another in puzzled terms what it is that makes this piece of God's earth so valuable, especially since it hardly yields them a living. Let us move to the Syrian-Israeli border, where soldiers, young people, women and men, guard on both sides and nervously finger their weapons, Soviet and American provided. On now to Sri Lanka, where ancient disputes and continued religious and caste consciousness fan the flames of distrust, and death is dealt daily to the innocent.

Now come with me across the ocean to Nicaragua. Let us go to the barrios and fabelas where the poor speak of freedom and dignity and God. From here they go out to fight filled with faith and free of fear, despite the power of their neighbors to the north. Let's go north to Washington, D.C., where decisions are made that affect the whole of the inhabited earth. Here people sleep in the streets, and young women die in childbirth, and old people freeze, and babies cry from hunger, and black people are set aside. And now to South Africa, to Soweto and Crossroads—that strange country where funerals are illegal and Christmas music is considered dangerous; where children are put in jail because they are determined to be free; where the strains of "How long, O Lord, how long, O Lord?" can be heard in the streets and in the churches.

Come with me to the maternity ward. The location could be any hospital, any birthing center anywhere in the world. In another few days I'll be there to wait for a new grandchild. We listen to the new babies cry and are touched again with the miracle of creation. New life makes new demands on us for a surer tomorrow.

Now, with these pictures in your mind, hear again the words of Isaiah, words of hope and promise and liberation . . .

> No more shall be heard in it the sound of weeping
>   and the cry of distress.
> No more shall there be in it
>   an infant that lives but a few days, . . .
> They shall build houses and inhabit them;
>   they shall plant vineyards and eat their fruit.
> They shall not build and another inhabit; . . .
> They shall not labor in vain,
>   or bear children for calamity; . . .
> They shall not hurt or destroy
>   in all my holy mountain.

Here is a vision where none are hungry or homeless or despairing or captive or lonely, a place where the tree of peace—whose roots are justice—flowers and bears the fruit of hope. Here is a vision where all know that here reside God's disciples, for the evidence of love is everywhere in this holy mountain. Here is God's future and we are called to bear witness to this future, in this time and in this place. God's future is not only the future of the end time, it is not only a vision but, if there is to be a tomorrow, God's future must become today's urgent agenda. It is toward this end that we seek to be a faithful church and loving disciples so that the world might see how we act and believe. The church is called to be a sign of the world God wills and an instrument of the Holy Spirit to bring into being such a world. Praise be to praxis for us!

It is what we do now that makes sense of what is to come. We are to bear witness to God's love and to God's future, no matter how inadequate we may feel. For the Scripture tells us that we can put our excuses aside, for God has given us power and the Holy Spirit is with us all of our days. This is God's gift to God's fearful people and God's call to faithfulness.

Let us be honest. What kind of witnesses have we been? Has our witness been worthy of the possibilities inherent in the power we have been given? Can we show to the world the evidence of a transforming force in this world? We must confess that injustice and poverty and the threat of annihilation do not hold up well as evidences of our seriousness in working toward God's future. Do we dare to be passionate about this future that God sets before us? We would not even have to ask this question if we were among the sisters and brothers that we visited at the beginning of this sermon. Our passion for a new world would be born of our suffering, for without the sweet hope of a holy mountain where none shall hurt or destroy we might die of despair.

Let me share with you the words of Allan Boesak because I think it may give you a sense of the kind of hope and passion that is inherent in many who struggle for their very lives. In Allan's new book *Comfort and Protest*, he writes to all of us who have joined in the struggle and says, "for all those who true to their faith have struggled and fought with us, have gone to jail, have shared pain and bread, they are seeing the power of the beast and they shall surely see the victory of the lamb." That is passion! But what about us and our passion for a new world? Can we who live where decisions are made daily that deal in the life and death for millions, be passionate about God's future? If we appear to be afraid of passion, there is good reason. A holy passion is a mix of joy with agony, of suffering with security, of love with betrayal. Passion crowds out fear. Faith is required to be passionate, for it

120

makes absolutely no sense in an affluent and increasingly secular society, a society where suffering and sacrifice are to be avoided (and if they cannot be avoided, they then must be hidden). But without sacrifice life loses volume and weight. An unbearable lightness of being is the outcome; and with a featherweight existence, *not only sacrifice but joy become impossible.* When passion is missing, death, not life, dominates. To be passionate is to risk suffering and to find joy. It may be the only way for the Spirit to enter our complacent souls. *God's love for us is not platonic!* We dare not offer less to those who share this planet with us. Possibly, just possibly, if we become passionate about God's future it will creep into all our acts of praise, and our work and our worship and our prayer life will be renewed and rekindled and we will be reborn.

How can we as Disciples, looking toward the 21st Century, bear witness in this risky present to God's future? There are many things that could be mentioned, but I choose to mention just two. First, let me confess that I come to you as a converted Disciple. My history is quite normal history for a "Disciple." I come out of a Presbyterian heritage, and my main claim to fame at the moment is that I have a grandson whose name is Alexander. How is that for a sterling credential? I find myself being introduced as the grandmother of Alexander Campbell.

There are two gifts that I perceive we bring from the past—our commitment to unity (no surprise on that from a professional ecumenist) and our affirmation of the Lord's Supper. The centrality of this feast of life, this supper to which the whole world is invited, is the root of our ecumenical vision and our global mission. It is the source of our identity, an identity that may well cause us to lay down our institutional life for our friends. We cannot bear witness alone, and our very smallness has saved us from that temptation.

Let us speak about the unity we seek. Every Disciple knows that Campbell set forth the premise that "the church is essentially, intentionally, and constitutionally one." History tells us that this statement created in our church a passion for unity or, at least, a lot of guilt about denominational chauvinism. What do you suppose would have happened if instead of saying what he did, he had said the people of God are essentially, intentionally, and spiritually (or maybe he would have said scripturally) one. Let me repeat it. The people of God are essentially, intentionally, and spiritually one. Would our ecumenical encounters and actions have been different?

Wonder we may, but that is not what he said. Our unity has for the most part, and I do not say this as a criticism but simply as reality, been focused on the church as institution. Our search has largely been for the organic unity of the churches. But in the late 1960s the third world gained influence in the World Council of Churches, the black churches began to make their voices heard in the Consultation on Church Union, and women—well, stepped out of the kitchen and into the pulpit. And we were forceably, passionately, as it were, brought face to face with the completeness and the fullness of the meaning of the word *unity*.

Raccoon John Smith tried to tell us this when he said, "God has put but one people on the earth and he exhorts them to be one family." This unity began to be spoken of in the WCC as the unity of the church and the unity of humankind. A new and more whole understanding of unity began to be understood and articulated. So perhaps we need a restatement of Campbell's premise. Why not claim *the church is intentionally, essentially, and constitutionally one and the people of God are spiritually bound together with the same essential and intentional oneness.* This is the dream of unity that will carry us into the 21st Century—a unity that deals seriously with diversity and inclusiveness and the inevitable sharing of power that must come if we are serious about those words. Unfortunately, to speak of diversity has become as easy as putting words on a Hallmark greeting card.

We can speak of unity as our polar star, but it will not carry the day unless we realize that racism and sexism and economic superiority and exploitation is part and parcel of our search for unity. The unity of the church and the renewal of our broken human community are inseparably bound into one. For those of us who claim the liberation struggle as our own, we must understand that programs against injustice are not put in place because someone in Geneva or Indianapolis or New York decreed it to be a priority but because Jesus Christ is Lord. It is not complicated: Where there is one shepherd there is one flock. The struggle for justice and righteousness is not a struggle of our making. It is not a struggle for noble ideals or lofty aspirations, but it is the struggle for an order of things that is surer than tomorrow's sunrise.

And we come to the Lord's table week after week to remember the familial relationship shared by all Christians. We are related to all our sisters and brothers in the world by the blood of Jesus and redeemed by his passion and his suffering. Communion is a very personal moment, but it is never a privatistic event. It is instead a covenant to be community with all of God's creation. In the Middle East there is a cultural tradition that instructs us in the meaning of sharing a meal. Now in the sophisticated times of today I don't suppose it is carried out fully, but there are still parts of the Middle East where tradition holds true. You don't accept an invitation to dinner in the Middle East easily because if you are invited to a person's home to share a meal with them you are considered part of that family. Not only are you invited but you are expected to call on that family forever for anything you might want—money, help, all that you might need. It was in this land with this tradition that Jesus invited his disciples to supper. It is in this same spirit that God invites all of God's children to the table. The commemorative aspects of the Lord's Supper, a looking back in the midst of the present, is always closely tied, in history and in Christian theology, to the eschatological dimension of the Supper. The people of God come to the table with the familial privileges, hosted by a God who showed his love for us on the cross and who expects us to love one another.

Because we lack clarity about the connection between unity and the Lord's Supper, history will unfortunately record that the table has been both a sign of our unity and an evidence of our disunity. Not only can Roman Catholics and Orthodox not come to the table with Protestants, but the table has been the place where our social sins have sought sanctification. Today in many places women cannot celebrate communion; people of color and whites cannot commune together in most of the churches in South Africa and don't in many churches here. Two hundred years ago when black people were relegated to slave balconies (and if you have never seen them you ought to visit one), they could not share the table with whites. This of course was a reflection of the society at large. Not sharing lunch counters was easy when even the Lord's Table was treated as exclusive property.

But there is another picture I carry in my mind, and some of you share this. It is the communion service at Vancouver, at the Sixth Assembly of the World Council of Churches. Here were

123

gathered, just as at all worldwide ecumenical gatherings, living witnesses from all corners of the earth. Their presence produced as it were a concentrate of all the situations of tension in the modern world. The people of the churches of South Africa, from Central America, from Asia, from Australia, from the Soviet Union, Rumania, East and West Germany, Sri Lanka, and more were there, making all those tragic situations vividly present. As always it highlighted the urgent need for universal solidarity of the Christian family. So they came, from the East and from the West, from the North and from the South, to partake together of the eucharist—that aperitif of the feast that is yet to come. The unity of the church and the renewal of the human community cannot be separated.

I would wish that this Christian Church (Disciples of Christ) might commission a creative, sensitive, and talented artist (now notice I did not say photographer, because this picture cannot be "taken"; it has to be created) to create for us a visual image, an icon as it were, to be placed in the sanctuary of every Disciples congregation in the world. Interesting, isn't it, that both the Orthodox, out of their ancient understanding of faith, and Madison Avenue are clear that visual images have power. I admit that an icon is not very "Disciples." But for the Orthodox an icon is a picture that is placed in time somewhere between Pentecost and the Eschaton. It is a picture of the future. We come to the Lord's Table with a picture in our mind, do we not? We come with a picture of the Last Supper, and that is quite appropriate, for it roots us in historical reality and calls us to remember. But I am suggesting that there might be added to that another image—one that sets before us God's future. Again, I think the setting ought to be a table (I wish we could call ourselves "people of the table" instead of "people of the parentheses"), a round table, for equality— a vision of the feast of life. The guests would be multicolored, and they would be from every culture. Women would be in abundance. No one would be able to tell who was rich or who was poor, and crutches and wheelchairs would be off to the side, and food would be plentiful and shared by all, and joy would abound. Children and the elderly would be welcome, and the table would be set in the midst of a lush and welcoming and safe and generous creation. Bread and wine and rice and coconut milk would be shared by all. No guns, no guards would be needed, and a loving

124

God would look upon God's earthly family, and their love for one another would be made incandescently clear. And we're made whole again.

We could hang the icon in a prominent place in proximity to the Lord's Table so that week after week we might be reminded that when we drink this cup and eat this bread we remember God's love for us and are called anew to love one another, to bear witness daily in very practical ways to God's future, to feed the hungry, to free the captive, to mend the brokenhearted, to end our warring madness and our faithless divisions, to seek peace, to sacrifice on behalf of a world transformed, and to be passionate in our love for one another.

> God. living breath in all flesh.
> your defenselessness often scares us,
> the ease with which you can be smothered.
>
> why have you
> made yourself
> and all life
> dependent on breath?
>
> a world made only out of breath!
> how easily it breathes its last!
>
> and so we pray
> at this time of fear:
> breathe your breath,
> the breath of the Holy Spirit,
> raise from the dead
> the future of the world
> the future of the churches.
>
> —Kurt Marti, "Whither Ecumenism?"